2008

D0956084

Praise for
21 Distinctions of Wealth

"It's time for you to attract all the wealth you want now by reading this great book and activating Peggy's perfect 'demandment.'"

— **Mark Victor Hansen,** the co-creator of the
#1 *New York Times* best-selling series *Chicken Soup for the Soul*®

"Abundance is your birthright . . . however, awareness is the key to attraction. I have watched Peggy McColl study, manifest, and teach this information for 25 years. If you want abundance, she can sure show you how to get it."

— **Bob Proctor,** the best-selling author of *You Were Born Rich*

"Peggy McColl has done it again! **21 Distinctions of Wealth** *seizes the essence of universal principles in a way that makes manifesting abundance simple, exciting, empowering, and notonly possible but probable. I highly recommend this book to anyone wanting a more prosperous future!"*

— **Crystal Andrus,** the best-selling
author of *Simply . . . Woman!*

*"***21 Distinctions of Wealth** *can help you to attract the abundance you deserve in your life, just as the subtitle says. Every one of us has the capability of creating a life of prosperity, abundance, happiness, and fulfillment. Peggy McColl's clear writing shows us the way. Read it carefully, work and play with it in your life—and prepare yourself for some truly remarkable results!"*

— **Marc Allen,** the author of *The Millionaire Course*
and *The Greatest Secret of All*

"In this brilliant book, Peggy McColl reveals the wisest and most profound principles to help you bring more wealth into every area of your life. Apply these principles today and be ready for an avalanche of abundance."

— **Marci Shimoff,** the #1 *New York Times* best-selling author of
Chicken Soup for the Woman's Soul and *Happy for
No Reason;* a featured teacher in *The Secret*

"This book is an instant classic! Simple, powerful, and brilliant. Peggy McColl teaches us how to bring more abundance into our lives, our relationships, and our world. I love this book."

— **Kurek Ashley,** the internationally best-selling
author of *How Would Love Respond?*

"Inspiring! In this great book, Peggy leads you through an easy process to experience more abundance in your life starting today! This may become your bible as you carry it with you everywhere and prosper in unimaginable ways."

— **Dr. Joe Vitale,** the author of *The Key* and *The Attractor Factor*

"Put these 21 Distinctions to work in your life, and watch the effortless, positive transformation begin to flow."

— **Gay Hendricks, Ph.D.,** the author of *Five Wishes: How Answering One Simple Question Can Make Your Dreams Come True* (**www.hendricks.com**)

"Peggy McColl's 21 Distinctions of Wealth offers truly inspiring advice on how to achieve real abundance in every arena of your life. You'll find yourself turning to it again and again for its practical techniques, life-altering insights, and motivating affirmations. This book will surely turn your energy around!"

— **Sandra Anne Taylor,** the *New York Times* best-selling author of *Quantum Success*

"Lots of people complain about a lack of wealth. Peggy McColl has done something about it. She has cut through the clutter and identified 21 Distinctions of Wealth that are available to each and every one of us. If you faithfully follow her plan, scarcity will melt away and you'll start attracting the abundance in your life that is your true destiny."

— **Steve Sanduski,** the *New York Times* best-selling author of *Avalanche: The 9 Principles for Uncovering True Wealth*

"Peggy McColl has created a phenomenal work that combines spirituality with a practical system to create and manifest wealth in your life. Her underlying philosophy penetrates our core and provides an enlightened view of success and wealth."

— **David Riklan,** the founder of **SelfGrowth.com,** the #1 self-improvement Website

"New York Times bestseller Peggy McColl's new book, 21 Distinctions of Wealth, is an essential resource for anyone who wants to wake up to experience the joyful abundance our world has to offer."

— **Robert McDowell,** the author of *Poetry as Spiritual Practice*

"If it's wealth you desire, read this book. Peggy McColl is an inspiring teacher and a self-made woman who is uniquely qualified to set you on the path to greater abundance in all areas of your life."

— **Debbie Ford,** the #1 *New York Times* best-selling author of *The Dark Side of the Light Chasers* and *Why Good People Do Bad Things*

21
Distinctions
OF
WEALTH

21 Distinctions OF WEALTH

ATTRACT THE **ABUNDANCE** YOU DESERVE

PEGGY McCOLL

HAY HOUSE, INC.
Carlsbad, California • New York City
London • Sydney • Johannesburg
Vancouver • Hong Kong • New Delhi

Published and distributed in the United States by: Hay House, Inc.: www.
hayhouse.com • **Published and distributed in Australia by:** Hay House
Australia Pty. Ltd.: www.hayhouse.com.au • **Published and distributed
in the United Kingdom by:** Hay House UK, Ltd.: www.hayhouse.co.uk •
Published and distributed in the Republic of South Africa by: Hay House
SA (Pty), Ltd.: www.hayhouse.co.za • **Distributed in Canada by:** Raincoast:
www.raincoast.com • **Published in India by:** Hay House Publishers India:
www.hayhouse.co.in

Editorial supervision: Jill Kramer   •   *Design:* Bryn Starr Best

Library of Congress Cataloging-in-Publication Data

McColl, Peggy
   21 distinctions of wealth : attract the abundance you deserve / Peggy
McColl.
      p. cm.
   ISBN-13: 978-1-4019-2007-4 (hardcover) 1. Self-actualization
(Psychology) 2. Quality of life. 3. Wealth. 4. Success. I. Title. II. Title:
Twenty-one distinctions of wealth.
   BF637.S4M23 2008
   332.024'01--dc22   2007043195

ISBN: 978-1-4019-2007-4

11 10 09 08   4 3 2 1
1st edition, May 2008

Printed in the United States of America

To my husband,
Denis

Contents

Introduction

21 DISTINCTIONS OF WEALTH

The dictionary defines a *distinction* as something that's different and bears the mark of excellence. When we say someone is a "man of distinction," we're expressing that he has something special that other men don't have. We remark, "How wonderful for him! But of course, I couldn't have what he has. I don't have his qualities . . . his style . . . his talents . . . his luck . . . his connections." Instead of sighing in envy, we can choose to develop the 21 Distinctions of Wealth that allow us to be different and to excel at manifesting abundance. These distinctions give us the power to create all the wealth we desire.

Many of the people I talk to in my work as a life coach tell me that they wish they could experience financial abundance. They speak of wealth as something far out of their reach, something that's not available to them and is reserved for a special group of people.

They can recite a long list of reasons why they can't have what they hope for and deserve. They don't realize that the only thing holding them back from achieving wealth is their own limited perceptions and beliefs.

The 21 Distinctions of Wealth are enormously powerful core beliefs held by those who experience abundance. When you truly believe in the 21 Distinctions, holding them in your heart and feeling their energy, you become a magnet for the wealth you seek. You draw to you that which you desire (the Law of Attraction).

It's not enough to merely read about these gold nuggets of wisdom. If you want to attract prosperity, you must change your thoughts, feelings, and actions and create wealth consciousness—an awareness of the nature of abundance and its flow. When you think and feel like a millionaire, you can *become* one.

In my previous book, *Your Destiny Switch*, I explained how you can create the life you desire by working with the power of emotions. As you work with the 21 Distinctions of Wealth, remember that positive emotions are the fuel for your dreams. Allow yourself to feel the full force of them as you think and read about wealth creation. (**Note:** Some of the anecdotes in this book are ones I used in *Your Destiny Switch*. I've included them here because they are strong examples of how your emotions affect your ability to manifest your desires.)

Each of the 21 Distinctions includes affirmations, which, when used properly, will turn up the volume on your positive emotions and actually change your vibrational energy, making you a magnet for money. The key is to move beyond merely reciting affirmations to truly *believing* them. If you don't, you might as well be reading from the phone book! When you say, "I am already rich. I was born that way!" you need to believe it with your whole heart and feel the surge of joy you create when you say the words. It's the energy of your emotions that helps you manifest your desires.

Affirmations are positive, declarative, and in the present tense, because when you express your desires in this way, you're able to easily create the emotion of abundance. Saying "It would be nice if I had money" creates a feeling of lack and tells the Universe that you don't have what you desire. Affirming "I *love* that I have wealth!" lets the Universe know that you're experiencing abundance, and it responds by sending you situations and circumstances that mirror what you're feeling.

The mind doesn't distinguish between reality and what you're "only" imagining. If you experience a strong sense of abundance and wealth as you imagine yourself depositing a million-dollar check in your bank account, you'll create the same vibration that you would if you were *actually* depositing it. So, to manifest wealth and abundance, you must believe that you already have what you want, and you must experience the happiness, satisfaction, enthusiasm, and generosity you would feel if your bank account reflected the bounty you're experiencing in your heart.

Many people have heard of the Law of Attraction and wonder why they can't simply decide what they want, think hard about getting it, and sit back and watch as it manifests in their lives. They don't understand that the Law of Attraction is based on *energy*. Emotions are a form of energy that's much more powerful than that of mere thoughts. When you *feel* wealthy, rich, and overflowing with abundance, you won't become upset and worry about your bills. Instead, you'll be energized and enthusiastic about generating money and opportunities for yourself. Creating wealth won't seem like work.

As you read about the 21 Distinctions, reflect on their wisdom and think about how they apply to your own life. Look at your own experiences of wealth and lack, and see if the 21 Distinctions shed any light on them. My guess is that you'll awaken to wisdom that you've had but not been aware of until now, and you'll start to truly understand how the Law of Attraction works.

How to Work the 21 Distinctions Program

It takes three weeks to establish a habit, so to begin attracting the wealth you deserve, you'll need to focus on each of the 21 Distinctions for 21 days. The great news is that you only need to spend a few minutes daily working the program: in the morning when you first wake up, once during the day, and in the evening just before bedtime. However, it's very important that you not rush through the list of affirmations at the end of each chapter, reciting them quickly. You must devote whatever time it takes to genuinely believe them as you're speaking them. For some, it may take only a minute to create powerful emotions of abundance and gratitude; for others, it may take several minutes.

At the end of this book, you'll find a handy checklist for recording that you've recited your affirmations three times during the course of the day. The entire program will take 441 days, or just over a year, to complete. By then, you'll have truly internalized all 21 Distinctions.

Begin the program the morning after you've finished reading this book. After you wake up, reread the text describing the first Distinction of Wealth. Then, write out the affirmations at the end of the chapter; retype them on your computer, print them out, and photocopy them; or download a document containing the affirmations and checklist from my Website: **www.destinies.com**. Alternatively, you might commit to carrying this book with you wherever you go and using the affirmations list and the checklist provided at the back of the book. Whatever you do, set yourself up for success by establishing how you want to work with the affirmations and checklist, and then follow through consistently. Then, too, feel free to adjust these affirmations to make them even more powerful and personal, but remember that to be the most effective, they should always be positive and in the present tense.

Before you say your affirmations, take a few deep, slow breaths and become quiet. Breathe in very slowly and exhale very slowly. Do this a few times, because it will ease your thoughts and allow you to be in a focused, relaxed, and open state. Don't think about time or permit yourself to be distracted. Let all your other thoughts drift away for the moment so that you can be fully present to do your affirmation work.

Then, when you feel quiet, calm, and focused, begin to recite the affirmations for the Distinction you're working on. When you say an affirmation such as "I am open and receptive to wealth," meditate on it. Truly listen to the words. Feel their power. If they don't resonate in your heart and you find yourself thinking, *I don't believe this,* or *I wish that were the case, but it isn't—at least not for me,* that's okay. Don't judge yourself or give up. You simply have to keep working at believing them until they feel true. It may take several repetitions to get past your distractions and doubts, but you have the power to believe the words and experience the positive emotions that your belief will generate.

As you speak your affirmations aloud, allow yourself to experience lightness in your body and a surge of excitement coursing through you as you feel yourself believing what you're saying. Keep repeating the words until all doubt is erased from your heart.

Allow your mind to form pictures of what you're creating. As you generate the feeling of being open and receptive to wealth, you may envision yourself smiling as you sign the back of a large check that's made out to you, or opening your front door and receiving a valuable package from the mail carrier.

You might envision gold coins pouring down from the sky, showering you with riches as you stretch out your hands and even more coins spring forth from your palms. If you have a dream about wealth as you're working on this program, you might want to use the images found therein. Picture them in your mind while you're doing your daily work of saying your affirmations and believing in them.

Many people associate abundance and wealth with the color green, which reminds them of money, trees, and grass; or gold, the color of the sunshine that nourishes all life, as well as the precious metal that people have valued for thousands of years. You might envision rich, fertile soil and plants stretching toward the sky; a waterfall pouring abundance on you; or a big, open home filled with sunlight, opulent furnishings, and loving friends who surround you. If no images come to mind as you say your affirmations, don't worry. What's most important is to create the positive feelings that lead to manifesting wealth.

As you say the affirmations, you may want to use body movements to enhance your emotions. For example, when you say "I open my arms to wealth," spread your arms in a gesture of receiving.

You may find it helpful to alter the affirmation to make it easier for you to create the emotions you desire. Feel free to substitute "God" or "the Divine Creator" for "the Universe." Also, some words will resonate for you more than others. Here are a few that can create the feeling of abundance that you can use as substitutions in affirmations if you find them especially powerful for you:

opulent	flourishing
luxurious	thriving
lush	booming
fertile	blossoming
rich	bountiful
affluent	plentiful
lavish	saturated
wealthy	full
abundant	prosperous
flowing	copious
golden	teeming
verdant	overflowing
fertile	prodigious

After you've finished reciting your affirmations, record that you've done so, using the checklist at the back of this book or the one provided on my Website.

At some point in the middle of the day, repeat the process of slowing down, breathing deeply, and reciting your affirmations as many times as it takes to genuinely feel them. Before you retire for the night, say them again, for a total of three short sessions devoted to reading these statements aloud with tremendous emotion. Remember to record on the checklist that you've completed all three. Seeing the tangible evidence of your progress will inspire you to continue.

If you accidentally forget and miss a session, don't give up the program! In fact, even if you drop the program for a few days because you become distracted, don't judge yourself negatively and tell yourself, *Well, I blew it.* Get right back to it and continue with the Distinction again until you've worked on it for 21 days. You may want to reread the chapter for the Distinction you're working on halfway through the 21 days in order to refresh your memory about it.

One of the best ways to establish a habit is to tie it in to another habit that you've already developed. Early in the morning before you get distracted by all the events of your day, recite your affirmations as you're eating breakfast, grooming yourself in the bathroom, or getting ready to start your car. I like to keep my affirmations in a drawer in my bathroom vanity and take them out to read just after brushing my teeth. You might keep them clipped to the sun visor or in the glove compartment of your car, taped next to your bathroom mirror, or in the drawer next to your coffeemaker. In the middle of the day, you may want to pull your affirmations out of your wallet or purse and begin to recite them as you sit down to lunch, while you take a regular break in your workday, or when you're in your car outside your children's school waiting for them to come out of the building.

Again, find a handy place for keeping your list of the affirmations for the particular Distinction you're currently working on developing. Because routines can change unexpectedly, if you don't carry this book with you everywhere, keep extra copies of your affirmations at hand wherever you are—you might place copies in your car, in your purse, in your reading-glasses case, or on your desk. At the end of the evening, when you're feeling reflective and are letting go of all the thoughts, emotions, and activities you've engaged in, recite your affirmations again. Feel the words in your heart as you say them and know that what you vibrate you'll create.

Whenever negative thoughts or feelings about money and abundance drift into your head, or you start to believe that you can't have the wealth you desire and deserve, stop yourself. Pull out your affirmations and recite them with great feeling over and over until you feel your vibrational energy change. As you develop this habit, you'll start to see the Universe moving to bring you physical manifestations of all that wealth you're experiencing inside you. Open your heart and your arms . . . because you deserve to be rich!

Distinction #1

You Are Already Rich— You Were Born That Way!

Wealth is your birthright. It's *everyone's* birthright! The silver spoon was in your mouth on the day you were born. You may not realize it because you think that to have riches you need lots of cash or financial holdings—or a genuine silver spoon—but this is a very limited and distorted way of thinking about wealth. Being rich doesn't necessarily mean you have a pile of $100 bills, a stack of gold bars, or a mink coat in your closet.

What most people don't understand is that wealth is an energy force. Every one of us can tap into this wonderful force whenever we like because it comes from a Divine source of abundance that is always available to us. We're all born with access to this faucet of abundance. Turn it on and you'll find that wealth manifests in your life in many different ways: You may have plenty of friends and family, a treasure chest full of ideas, abundant joy and enthusiasm, and any number of expressions of affluence. When you develop the 21 Distinctions of Wealth, you'll know how to turn on that faucet.

A major reason why most of us block the flow of wealth and abundance is that we get stuck on the details of how it shows up in our lives. This blinds us to the creativity of the Universe, which has far more clever ideas about how to manifest riches than we can possibly imagine. We insist that we want cash or gold, but really, what good is a stack of green paper or a bar of gold? What can you do with them? I suppose that you could use a bar of gold as a paperweight or to prop a door open, and you might use a piece of that green paper to mark your place in this book. Currency, precious metals, jewels, and fur aren't wealth; they're merely *symbols* of it, representing something of value that can be exchanged for something else of value. If you recognize all the forms of wealth available to you, you can start trading them in for what *you* most value.

Right this moment, you may be extremely wealthy and not even realize it. Everyone has a great deal of value, or assets, that they can enjoy and increase. You probably don't have stacks of bills or gold bars lying around your home, but I'm certain that you have a personal hidden gold mine you can work with and turn into another form of wealth. Your gold is special because unlike the precious metal, it's magnetic. Once you recognize it, value it, feel gratitude for it, and experience the joy of possessing it, you'll find that your gold is vibrating and acting as a magnet, attracting even more wealth to you.

Do you doubt that you have a hidden gold mine? Most of us focus on what we lack and overlook our special gifts, qualities, and resources—whether it's our creativity, our abundant love, our willingness to work hard, our excellent communication skills, our boundless enthusiasm, or some other quality or skill that has great value. Instead, we start subscribing to negative thinking and telling ourselves that we can't have wealth, that it's foolish to hope for it. These kinds of thoughts and the oppressive feelings they create blind us to the riches we hold within us.

In the 1930s, a ten-foot-tall clay statue of the Buddha, which had been found in a deserted Buddhist monastery, was moved into a storage facility. Twenty years later, monks at a monastery in Bangkok, Thailand, expressed a desire to own the statue of the great

Buddha, so arrangements were made to move it. But as it was being lifted, it slipped off the crane and fell. The giant Buddha cracked, and at first everyone felt terrible that this beautiful statue was ruined. But then the movers realized that peeking through the crack was a shimmer of gold. Upon investigation, they discovered that beneath the clay exterior was a solid-gold statue, which had been covered in mud centuries before in order to prevent robbers from recognizing its value and stealing it. After hundreds of years, none of the monks who knew the Buddha's secret remained. Those who had valued the statue for what it represented now discovered that it was a treasure in another sense: It was worth a fortune!

In your life, what golden Buddhas lie hidden beneath the mud? What qualities and resources have you forgotten about because you haven't considered just how valuable they are? What are your overlooked blessings? What do you possess that can be exchanged for what you most desire? You may be thinking, *I don't have what it takes to be wealthy. I don't have the right skills, the education, the connections, or the time to create wealth.* Yet if you look carefully, you might unearth talents, wisdom, qualities, resources, and ideas that are secretly worth a fortune.

Like everyone else, you were born with precious seeds of wealth . . . but have you claimed them, planted them, and nourished them? Some people are born with a knack for making friends and networking with other people—they might know the very individual who can direct them to where they need to be in order to receive the riches that are ready to flow into their lives. Others are tremendously creative and hardworking by nature, but they end up squandering precious time and never planting the seeds of their ideas in fertile ground. Still other people are brilliant observers and communicators who have the potential to transform those exceptional talents into another form of abundance.

If you're blind to the gold beneath the surface of your Buddha, it's because you lack the positive emotions that would open your eyes and allow you to rediscover and claim your birthright—emotions such as faith, confidence, worthiness, joy, enthusiasm, and abundance. Yes, abundance is an emotion. Feel it and experience it and your eyes will open to all the affluence already present in your life. Then you'll attract even more of it to you. Your wealth is there before you—ready to be claimed, invested, exchanged, built upon, and enjoyed.

Wealth truly is every human being's birthright. The Divine doesn't want us to go without. That's why we're born with curious minds; the potential to think, speak, and create something new; and open hearts that are willing to trust and believe in the seemingly impossible. Try telling a child that she can't possibly become a princess in a castle and she's likely to roll her eyes at how unimaginative and foolish you are. Much too quickly, we lose our ability to believe that we can live a life of opulence and luxury.

Look around at our world, lush with life and filled with strange and extraordinary creatures who remind us that the "impossible" is possible. (I once read that honeybees aren't supposed to be able to fly according to the laws of aerodynamics, but they do it anyway!) Think of the millions of microscopic creatures and countless leaves on all the trees in the world. What makes us think there isn't enough abundance to go around? Human beings in the most primitive living conditions have created art, music, tools, and new ideas and found resources to draw upon. The Divine gave us the ability to conceive and create, to think and to dream. So why don't we believe we can manifest what we desire?

As a goal-achievement coach, I've met many people who are held back from creating the lives of their dreams because of their strong negative feelings that actually block them from manifesting and receiving the riches they deserve. They generate the emotions of lack and guilt and lose faith that the Universe is there to co-create with them all that they long for. Their bodies actually create an energetic vibration that attracts people and situations mirroring their belief that they're lacking. They readily give up their birthright of abundance and creativity, as if it had no value, and leave behind their childlike willingness to dream and believe. Their resourcefulness slips away, and they can't recognize the wealth that's inside and all around them, just waiting to be claimed by them.

When my son, Michel, was 12, he would often take apart broken skateboards that he found in the garbage at a skateboard park. What another person saw as junk he had the creativity to view as a source of wealth. He would clean up the pieces—the wheels and such—and sell them as replacement parts to the kids at school. He then exchanged the money he made for fishing gear or accessories for his mountain bike. He, like so many children and young people, hasn't lost his ability to see the gold inside the Buddha. He recognizes the wealth around him and the resources he has within, such as his knowledge about skateboards and his cleverness. With the eyes of a child, he can recognize riches when he sees them and claim them for himself, without guilt or embarrassment.

You, too, have this ability to reclaim your birthright and start living a prosperous, abundant life. All you have to do is let go of the negative thoughts and feelings that have been blocking you and open yourself up to the gifts you were born with.

A shimmering, golden fortune is mine.

Wealth flows into me like a fertile river, nurturing me, enriching me, and helping me produce all that I desire.

Inside me is sheer opulence. I am filled with riches, teeming with possibilities. My tremendous wealth is flowing forth, nourishing my life and nourishing everyone around me.

I have always had all the wealth that I need. I savor the riches that are my birthright.

Distinction #2

THE WILLINGNESS TO GIVE IT ALL UP
LEADS TO HAVING IT ALL

When I first heard Deepak Chopra talk about this Distinction of Wealth, I couldn't imagine how it might be true. I'd worked very hard for my money and for all that I owned. I was a single mother with no college education, yet I had a lovely house, a nice car, a flourishing consulting business, and money in the bank. How could I possibly give it all up? And why should I?

Then my business took a downturn, which is part of the natural cycle of wealth. Prosperity is like nature because it has several seasons: There's a time for planting, for tending our garden, for harvesting all that we've grown, and for rest and reflection as we prepare for another period of growth. I became scared and resisted this wintertime. I didn't trust its quietness or see that it was providing me with an opportunity for indulging in the creative process and planning my spring garden. I didn't want quiet—I wanted the phone to ring off the hook as clients clamored for my services! I wanted to be very busy and distracted by lots and lots of work and trips to the bank to deposit my hefty paychecks. I longed to watch my business grow upward at a nonstop rapid pace, generating more and more and more money.

The thought of having no income made me feel very anxious. I had a little boy to support. I had an assistant who depended on me for *her* income, and I'd paid her more in the previous year than I'd been able to pay myself in salary. My finances were dwindling, and I was terrified.

My fear told my mind: *Work harder!* I figured that if I put my head down and spent hours upon hours at the office, I could pull myself out of the financial hole I was digging. In the meantime, I couldn't bring myself to pull back on my spending. I felt that if I did, it would be a reminder that I didn't have the money I usually had, and that would send me into a new spiral of panic as I started creating negative thoughts about my ability to turn my financial situation around. I was overspending out of fear and lack.

Then one day I listened to a Deepak Chopra audiotape and heard him say that to have it all, you have to be willing to give it all up. Although I'd heard this tape before and I still didn't understand exactly what he meant, now I was so frazzled and worried by my situation that I started thinking more about what he was saying. Somehow I sensed that it was important to take in his wisdom and try to apply it to my life.

The more I pondered what he'd said, the more I began to understand this Distinction of Wealth. My fear of losing what I had was driving my frantic scrambling to bring in business. I came to realize that if I could let go of the fear and trust that money would come in, I could open myself up to a range of positive emotions that would help me create the wealth I desired. I've always known that emotions are enormously powerful, and I was starting to understand that positive ones have the power to put us back on track to being creative, flexible, confident, and open to new possibilities that we might be missing. I certainly wasn't in a creative state of mind with so much fear swirling around inside of me!

I began to imagine what I might be able to manifest if I let go of my fear of losing it all, and I concentrated on creating positive emotions. I could begin to have faith and confidence. I was able to experience tranquility and quiet. In that peaceful stillness, bolstered by my trust in myself and in things unseen, I could open myself up to all the opportunities I'd been overlooking when I was focusing my mind on my fears and my bottom line and creating fear.

I started to realize that by generating positive emotions, I was effortlessly contracting my spending without giving in to fear. I wasn't hoarding my money; rather, I was simply and naturally purchasing less and feeling great about the sense of control I had over my emotions, my spending, and my life.

I started to envision a lush garden of wealth that would allow me to live the way I wanted to live. I pictured myself paying my bills easily and talking on the phone to new clients. I savored the awareness that I could afford to maintain a beautiful home for my son and myself in the safe, friendly neighborhood where we lived, and I felt my happiness at knowing I could easily pay for his private schooling. I imagined myself helping clients achieve their own goals as they paid me a good, fair price for my services, allowing me to run my business smoothly and pay my excellent assistant. I pictured my financial fortunes turning around and moving in the other direction—up toward the sky!—

and experienced excitement and joy as I did so. I let go of my fears that I might lose all that I'd worked for, and gave up my habit of feeling lack.

I recognized that if I'd been able to manifest the wealth I had in my life once, even if I lost it all, I could create it again. There was no reason to hold on to fear. If I had to sell my house, I could buy another someday, and it might be one I loved even more. If my business went under, I would be okay, because I have the ability to reinvent myself—and maybe my new career would be even more lucrative.

I began to feel faith, confidence, calm, and happiness. These feelings changed my vibrational energy, and I found I was starting to draw into my life the opportunities and wealth I desired. Creative ideas came to me, and I felt enthusiastic and eager to implement them. My seeds turned into seedlings, then blossomed and flourished . . . and before I knew it, I had a bountiful harvest again.

When we hold on to the external manifestations of wealth, and give in to a fear of losing them, we create the energy of lack and actually drive away our prosperity. Money slips through our fingers, opportunities dry up, and our resources become more deeply buried and hidden from sight. We lose what we have, become more fearful, and fall deeper into the hole of want. But if we stop ourselves and let go of our fears and our attachments to what we have right now, we open ourselves up to building even more wealth than we ever dreamed we could have.

Are you able to enjoy your money and have faith that you can increase it, or are you fearful of losing it, constantly checking your bank accounts and worrying about tomorrow? Does the smallest downturn in your fortunes cause you to panic? Let go of your attachments to how and when your wealth will come to you. You know what you've planted. Be patient and have faith that your efforts will bear fruit. Acknowledge your skills as a gardener, and be confident in your ability to tend your crop. Release fear . . . and the need to control. Then wealth will come to you naturally and easily.

My wealth takes many forms. I tend a beautiful, lush garden that bursts into bloom in the sunshine. I have faith that I am growing richer every day in many ways.

Abundance and prosperity are always available to me. I have complete confidence in my ability to foster and create wealth. I am always wealthy.

Riches flow into my life. I allow them to come
to me from all directions, to wash over me, and
to fill me up. I am saturated with wealth.

I allow abundance to pour into my life, and I open myself
to the Universe's bounty. Wealth comes to me at the exact
time I need it. I have as much money as I need, and more.

Distinction #3

THERE IS AN INFINITE
SUPPLY OF ABUNDANCE

Between the moment you're born and the moment you die, you'll take about 400 million breaths. Are you counting them? How many have you taken so far?

Naturally, we don't pay attention to the number of breaths we take because we simply assume that each time we inhale, there will be air available for us. When it comes to abundance, however, many of us develop a lack mentality because we assume that there's a limited supply of resources in the Universe. Like air, though, abundance is continually flowing in and out, in and out. And just as when we're anxious, we begin breathing shallowly, restricting our airflow, we obstruct our stream of wealth when we start to think, *There might not be enough for me!*

Often when I lecture, I bring an old-fashioned oil lamp with me, and I tell my audience to imagine it's

Aladdin's lamp. I ask them what they would wish for, and inevitably they make three wishes. They assume that, like Aladdin, they're only allowed three. My question is: *Why not make the third one be a wish for an unlimited number of wishes?* That way, they'd never run out of them. Why should we limit our desires if the Universe has boundless abundance?

Maybe you were taught not to be greedy and ask for too much, but did it ever occur to you that the desire to have more doesn't always come from greed? You might want more so that you can share even greater wealth with others. Many people say that if they were to win the lottery, the first thing they'd do is buy something for their aging parents and their best friends—the people who have given them unconditional love. It's not that they feel an obligation to pay back all the affection that was lavished upon them so generously; rather, it's that their hearts long to see those they care about experience feelings of joy, delight, and security.

Recently, I found out that a young person I know, the son of one of my friends, was struggling financially. He's a hardworking, wonderful young man, and I felt terrific about being able to give him a large sum of money, with no expectation of being paid back, to make his life a little easier. I think I enjoyed giving the gift as much as he enjoyed receiving it. The more money I have, the more I can let it flow forth from me out into the world again.

When you experience wealth consciousness—truly believing that affluence is an ever-flowing river that can be channeled and directed through the power of positive emotions—you find that you don't have feelings of greed, guilt, or lack. Instead, you feel fertile, giving, and generous as your cup overflows with joy and abundance. But when you have a lack mentality instead of wealth consciousness, you're fearful about how money is spent because you think there isn't enough to go around. Some people have a great deal of money but are constantly afraid of losing it and refuse to invest it, give any of it away, or risk any of it because they're afraid they won't have enough for a rainy day. They're frugal to the point of hoarding.

When we give freely and unconditionally, trusting in the infinite supply of abundance, we'll find that we have what we need. The love we share, the value we give others, and the bounty that we let flow from ourselves into the world will always come back around to us in some form or another.

There's a wonderful story in the novel *A Tree Grows in Brooklyn* that illustrates the importance of feeling the emotion of abundance in the face of scarcity. Katie Nolan is a poor mother in Brooklyn, New York, in the early 1900s. Although money is extremely tight and the family often goes hungry, she pours her daughter, Francie, a cup of coffee every morning—even though the girl never drinks from it. Francie savors the rich smell and the comforting warmth of the mug as she nestles it in her hand. She takes the time to enjoy her coffee every morning, and then when it has cooled off and she has finished drinking in its delicious smell and warmth, she pours the liquid down the drain. Katie says that she wants her daughter to know what it's like to experience the luxury of always having plenty to eat or drink in the house and being able to "waste" something. She believes that this teaches Francie what it would feel like not to be pinching every penny, afraid of squandering anything.

I'm not suggesting that you become wasteful, but I do want you to appreciate the wealth you have and create the emotions of gratitude and abundance about it. Think about whether your fear that there isn't "enough" in the world blocks you from truly enjoying your riches. Do you appreciate your warm, safe home . . . or do you continually feel bad that someone else is without such a nice place to live? Feeling guilty does absolutely nothing to help anyone else create abundance. Experiencing appreciation and gratitude, however, will turn up the volume on your other positive feelings and allow you to tap into the Divine source of creativity, and you'll be inspired to find ways to share your wealth with others.

There are many ways to channel the flow of plenitude so that it rushes into the lives of other people. You can give to charity, engage in a service project in your community, and take advantage of opportunities to help others. There are wonderful microfinancing organizations dedicated to lending money to entrepreneurs all over the world who have a great idea, enthusiasm, a business plan, and a willingness to build upon whatever capital they receive. When they succeed, they pay back the loan with interest so that someone else can have the resources to make their own dream of increasing abundance come true. Often these entrepreneurs need only a few hundred dollars to get started or to grow their businesses. People who want to help can contribute as little as $25.

We tend to think that we need an enormous amount of resources to create wealth, but that simply isn't true. It doesn't matter how much we have at the moment, because we can always grow it. Ultimately, there will always be "enough" for us and for everyone else. Once we let go of the idea that in order to feel affluent instead of lacking, we must have a checking account with an enormous sum of cash available to us, we start to discover all the other wonderful resources available to us.

I read in the newspaper that resourceful kids will buy bottles of water at discount stores, cool them in their family refrigerator, and sell them on the street for a large profit to passersby and drivers who are willing to pay for the convenience of a cold drink. They may have only a small amount of money to invest, but these kids realize that there will always be plenty of people who are thirsty on a hot summer day. Their resourcefulness allows them to grow their wealth.

And the father of a young man named Jared McBeth wrote to me to tell me about his son's cleverness: Jared was given a truck worth $2,500 when he was 16. He educated himself about cars and automotive engineering and scoured the used-car ads, and this allowed him to trade that truck for another vehicle, then another, then another—always trading up toward a better one—until now, six years later, he owns a BMW M Roadster sports car. Jared invested his time into growing his inner resources of knowledge and passion for cars, enhancing his inner gold so that he could magnetically attract better and better ones.

Let go of your fears that there isn't "enough" in the world and you'll start noticing all the resources you have around and inside you. Allow yourself to not only notice the abundance that's already present in your life, but also to bask in it, just as Francie Nolan savored her coffee each morning. Create a feeling of prosperity and you'll connect to the unlimited store of abundance available to you.

One of the best ways to create a powerful feeling of wealth and affluence is through visualization. I like to imagine being immersed in a green waterfall (green is the color of plants, so it symbolizes abundance and fertility). I can sense the power of the bright green water as it rushes over me and imagine it filling me with its riches. I feel the liquid move through me, out my fingertips, and pour itself onto the rich brown earth, which soaks it up and brings forth seedlings that grow and grow, stretching upward into the sky.

As I hold this vision and this sensation of drawing in wealth and sending it outward again, I recite my affirmations about prosperity with great feeling and enthusiasm. I breathe deeply and feel gratitude for the air that's always available to me. I'm thankful for the wealth that continually flows into me, through me, and out of me, connecting me with all the abundance in the Universe.

The fertile waters of wealth flow into me, through me, out of me, and back into me, connecting me with all the abundance in the Universe. I savor these waters. I drink deeply from the spring of abundance, and I feel nourished. I am saturated and overflowing with riches.

I breathe in and fill myself with all the abundance the Universe has available to me. Naturally, easily, I draw in the wealth I deserve. I express my prosperity, giving freely, with love and enthusiasm. I have plenty. I am blessed with riches. Money pours into my life, and I share my riches with the world. I love being wealthy.

Distinction #4

THE UNIVERSE IS ALWAYS GIVING

One day when I was a teenager and the senior prom was looming on the horizon, a friend and I were in a department store when she decided that we should try on prom dresses—and not just any prom dresses: She wanted to check out the dresses on the designer floor of the store.

My boyfriend had broken up with me earlier in the year, I hadn't been asked to the prom, and I knew that I didn't have the money for a fancy dress. I felt guilty and sad as I followed her to the designer floor, where she pulled several beautiful long gowns off the rack and headed for the dressing room.

"Do you really have enough money to pay for any of these dresses?" I asked my friend.

"Of course not!" she said. "I just want to see how I look in them. There's no harm in that."

"But . . . if you can't afford it, and no one's asked you to the dance—"

She waved her hand at me. "So what? Maybe someone will."

I never did go to prom, although my friend did—in a very pretty dress from one of the lower floors of that department store. At the time, I didn't understand that by allowing herself to feel entitled to a designer dress and a wonderful boy to take her to the dance, my friend was working with the Universe to co-create what she wanted for herself. The Universe responded because it wants us to have all we desire, it has an unlimited supply of abundance, and it's always giving. We just have to be willing to accept its gifts. We're open to receiving when we're experiencing the positive feelings of abundance and worthiness.

As I got older and began to travel, I started to realize that there's an enormous amount of wealth in the world. For the first time, I was exposed to beautiful, luxurious buildings and homes and expensive sports cars. I began to meet people who didn't blink at spending $200 on dinner and who vacationed in exotic places. The more I learned about the Law of Attraction—our ability to draw to us all that we desire by creating a vibration of attraction—the more I began to create the emotions that I'd experience if I had all that I wanted. With great feeling, I recited affirmations about having wealth. In my heart, I truly believed what I was saying when I stated aloud: "I am rich beyond my wildest dreams."

Whenever I caught myself looking at some luxury item and thinking, *That looks wonderful, and it's too bad I can't have it,* I'd stop myself. I now recognized that like everyone else, I have a right to enjoy prosperity. I'd begin to imagine owning that item, created the feelings that would go along with being in possession of it, and trusted that the Universe would bring that item to me or bless me with riches in some other way.

The more positive my feelings were, the more inspired I was to put forth the effort to grow my abundance. I made money, invested well, began a successful business, and enjoyed watching it blossom. It took time and hard work to get where I am today, but I now enjoy a life that's rich in many ways. I have an overflow of love and affection, self-acceptance, enthusiasm, humor, and confidence. I also have more traditional manifestations of wealth: a nice, large, beautiful home with a pool; a luxury vehicle I truly enjoy driving; and investments that grow every day. The Universe always had these gifts available. It was my own negativity that was blocking it from giving them to me.

Do you doubt that the Universe wants to bestow the gift of great abundance on you? When you see a sign on a construction site that says COMING SOON! LUXURY CONDOS STARTING AT $800,000! or you spot an expensive car in front of you on the highway, what feeling comes up for you? Is it one of lack, depression, or envy? If so, you're blocking yourself from attracting the wealth you desire.

Try this experiment: Test-drive a sports car, have a drink in the lobby of a luxury hotel, or try on an outrageously expensive outfit in a fancy boutique. As you do so, deliberately push aside any feelings of guilt or unworthiness. Create emotions of joy, enthusiasm, and gratitude. Isn't it wonderful that you can experience such luxury? Take pleasure in every moment, and affirm to yourself that you're entitled to all the riches you see around you. The car and the outfit may not be yours to take home yet—and your abundance may appear in a different form than the one you're enjoying at the moment—but your wealth will begin to manifest itself.

During the Great Depression, Hollywood movies featuring glamorous ladies in silk and furs and gentlemen in top hats and tuxedos enjoying opulent life-styles were enormously popular. People wanted to stay connected to the feeling of abundance, and for a few cents and a couple of hours, these movies allowed them to experience it easily and to let go of their emotions of lack and fear. Don't underestimate the power of the feeling of abundance! Revel in the thrill of walking through a luxury home that's been opened to the public. Page through magazines on luxury living, such as *Architectural Digest,* and envision that you live in one of the gorgeous houses they feature in their photographs. Feel entitled to a life of affluence, and open yourself to all the gifts the Universe wants to give to you.

I know that for many people, creating feelings of worthiness and entitlement can be very challenging. I used to feel awful about myself. I had a lot of difficulties as a child and teenager, and it took me a long time to believe that I deserved happiness, love, and prosperity. Even when I came to understand in my mind that I had a right to all that I desired, it was hard for me to hold on to that belief and feel it in my heart. If someone criticized me or treated me badly, or if I made a mistake or didn't live up to my standards of behavior, I spiraled downward into negative emotions.

I felt unworthy, guilty, sad, and angry at myself.

I had to learn that the point of negative feelings is to experience just enough suffering to wake us up to how we're blocking ourselves from receiving the gifts the Universe wants to bestow on us. I started to explore why I didn't feel good about myself—why I felt guilty or ashamed—and once I did, I realized that I was judging myself according to some values I didn't truly believe in. If you asked me, "Does everyone deserve to be happy and prosperous?" I'd say, "Yes, of course!" And yet here I'd singled myself out as someone who *wasn't* entitled to feel those emotions.

I eventually figured out why I'd created feelings of low self-esteem and unworthiness as a child, and I recognized that I didn't have to feel that way anymore. I made up my mind to stop re-creating these negative emotions in my life as an adult, because they weren't serving me. Every time I caught myself feeling unworthy, I observed what I was doing, stopped judging myself, and simply decided, *I don't like this feeling, and I'm going to feel something positive instead.* Then I switched into worthiness, abundance, joy, or faith, imagining what it would feel like to experience that emotion, and imagining so well that I actually *created* it.

When you switch out of negativity, it doesn't matter which positive emotion you choose to switch into because every one of them has the power to lift you out of fear, guilt, and other dark feelings and into positivity. Each positive emotion raises the level of your other positive emotions and causes you to feel deserving of the gifts the Universe has ready for you.

One of my favorite strategies for switching out of negativity is to wave my hands in front of me as if I were pushing away a cloud of smoke. Then I'll close my eyes, take a deep breath, and ask myself, *What emotion would I like to feel right now?* Whatever it is, I'll access a memory or an imaginary scene that has the power to create it in me. If I need confidence, I'll remember an occasion when I was confident and create in my mind a little film clip of what I was doing at the time. I relive my moment of confidence and re-create that feeling. (If you've never felt a particular emotion, you can imagine what it *might* feel like and envision a scene in which you're experiencing it.)

Right now, I want you to recollect a time when the Universe was giving to you and you felt rich and abundant. Maybe it was when you were enjoying sitting on your newly delivered sofa for the first time, running your hands along the material, feeling tremendous abundance as you enjoyed your purchase and your ability to pay for it. Maybe it was when you were a child and you came home from the drugstore with a bagful of candy that you bought with your allowance and you reveled in the thought that you could enjoy all those goodies. Perhaps you recall sitting around a table with many of your closest friends and family members, laughing at a joke together, enjoying all the wonderful food you were sharing, and feeling rich with love.

Hold this film clip of abundance in your mind's eye and play it over and over again, feeling your sense of abundance rise up inside you. In this moment, you're not just feeling rich—you're also sending a clear message to the Universe that you're ready to receive all the gifts of wealth it wants to give you. Open your heart to accept them.

What an incredible bounty I am enjoying! The Universe is overflowing with gifts for me. I hear the knocking at the door, and I open it to receive a shower of prosperity. I open my arms and receive all the gifts of the Universe with gratitude, enthusiasm, and joy. I feel lucky!

I am delighted to see all that the Universe has for me!
My wealth comes in many forms. The Universe
knows just what I need and brings abundance
in an infinite number of ways.

I am worthy of prosperity and abundance. I deserve
the best of the best, and I am deeply grateful for all my
wealth. I love experiencing the abundance that belongs
to me. I am the owner of the finest, most wonderful
home. I dine on the most delicious meals every day.
I savor every bite. I am deeply thankful for the oppor-
tunities and choices that I have and for my freedom.
I am deeply thankful for the abundance of love in
my life. I deserve to be rich! I _am_ rich!

Distinction #5

WHEN YOU LET GO OF ENVY, YOU LET GO OF IGNORANCE

Not long ago, one of my clients brought her mother to hear me speak at a workshop on goal achievement. She felt certain that if her mom heard what I had to say about abundance and wealth consciousness, the older woman would let go of her fears about money and start seeing how she could generate riches in her life. After my talk, my client's mother turned to her and said, "Peggy is just wonderful. I envy her. She's really one of those special, chosen people. No wonder she's a success."

When my client told me this story, I was surprised. I don't believe for a minute that my own prosperity is the result of my being "special" or "lucky." I was born with wealth and value, just as everyone else is, but I wasn't singled out by the Universe as one of the "rare few" who deserve success. The reason I'm wealthy is that I'm willing to regularly create positive feelings that fuel my ability to build upon the abundance I have.

Every day, I choose to create a feeling of gratitude and notice and value all that I possess already. I maintain faith in my ability to retain the wealth I have and also to manifest even more riches. I create enthusiasm, which gives me the energy to work hard—as well as curiosity, which helps me explore all the possibilities for wealth creation that are available to me. I trust that the Universe is always giving . . . not just to other people, but to *me.* My job is to be open to its gifts and to receive them with gratitude, grace, and enthusiasm.

Too often people will think, *There's a lot of wealth in the world, but it's not available to me.* At the root of envy is the mistaken belief: *That person has something I can't have.* But the Universe gives to everyone, including you. You can have what you desire. You have the power to attract wealth.

Maybe you have negative beliefs and feelings about yourself, such as *I'm unworthy of wealth,* or *I can't be trusted with money—I'm not smart enough to handle it.* You could be standing at the doorway to riches but be so convinced you don't have the power to open the door that you won't even try the knob. Instead, you look at others who are experiencing great prosperity and say, "Why can't I have that?" and create a feeling of envy that keeps you from opening the door to wealth.

Maybe you feel that the Universe sits on abundance, choosing only a few select people to enjoy the fruits of wealth. If so, you might want to explore why you think and feel that way.

Sometimes the belief *I can't have what I want,* one that causes envy, stems from what we learned from the people around us. Well-meaning family members, neighbors, and friends may try to protect those they love from being hurt by urging them not to dream too big. They don't realize that they're preventing them from claiming all the riches the Universe wants to give them.

Some people who care about you may feel threatened or abandoned when you start to experience affluence, and they'll withdraw their support and approval. They'll say you're not "authentic" anymore, or that you're acting as if you belong to another group of people. They say these things because they're buying into the false notion that their own group isn't entitled to abundance, and they're uncomfortable with the fact that someone else in the group is gaining wealth. They create feelings of lack and jealousy.

If this happens to you, be compassionate for those who try to hold you back and encourage them to believe they, too, can raise themselves up and live a life of plenty. If they can't generate faith, abundance, and worthiness in themselves, bless them—but don't let them convince *you* to create feelings of unworthiness. You're entitled to wealth, and you'll attract people who love and accept you as an affluent person whose riches are growing every day.

Maybe, regardless of what others think, you don't feel that the Universe will give to you because you believe that you're not worthy of receiving wealth. Feelings of low self-esteem left over from childhood can be very painful, but you need to replace them with positive assessments of yourself so that you can prosper. Every day, create the feeling and belief that you *are* worthy of an abundant life. You deserve wealth as much as anyone else does.

Often, our sense that the Universe doesn't have enough to go around causes us to become competitive in addition to envious. We forget that the Universe has abundant provisions and is always giving. We start to feel that if someone else is enjoying prosperity, he or she must be taking away from us and depleting the short supply. Now, it's true that there won't be enough to go around if we're fixated on achieving one very specific form of wealth when we all want it. There's a funny movie starring Arnold Schwarzenegger called *Jingle All the Way,* about two dads who go into intense competition to acquire a very rare action figure for their sons, and they practically wage war against each other rather than stepping back and asking, *I wonder if there's something else of value I could give to my son this Christmas—such as my love, my presence, and my undivided attention?* When we let go of our narrow ideas about what has value and about what we need in order to feel wealthy, we stop feeling that we have to claw and fight for riches in this world.

People who are ignorant of their own ability to create abundance will give in to envy and often begin looking for a rescuer, patron, or "sugar daddy" because they can't imagine how they can make money and create wealth on their own. They start to believe that in order to experience riches, they have to give up something—whether it's their independence or their freedom to speak their mind (because if they do speak up, they might offend the person who is financially supporting them). Their feelings of envy and resentment increase when they can't find someone to support them financially or to fix their money problems, and they fall deeper into the hole of negativity.

Whenever you find yourself envious, think of it as a warning bell going off. Step back from your jealousy, and without judging yourself as "bad" for feeling this negative emotion, simply explore why you think you can't have what the other person has. If you uncover a conviction that you're unworthy or that the Universe has a limited supply and only doles out its riches to those who lead a "charmed life" or who are more important or special than you are, get rid of that belief right now! Affirm your birthright to wealth.

If you look beneath your envy and uncover the belief *I can't have that because it's out of my reach financially,* then ask yourself, *What is it about that car, that home, or that lifestyle* [or whatever it is you're coveting] *that makes me want it so much?* Maybe it will be a long time before you have a Jaguar or a Porsche in your driveway, but what does that car mean to you? What does it symbolize? Can you find a way to experience the exhilaration of driving a fast car without owning one right now? Does the car symbolize importance, or sexiness? Why would you need a car to make you feel important and sexy?

If you create feelings of self-love, sexiness, and exhilaration in yourself, you'll have a Jaguar and

Porsche vibration. Maybe you'll get the car and maybe you won't, but it will feel terrific to experience those feelings and to know that the Universe is responding to them by changing the circumstances around you to reflect your self-love, sexiness, and exhilaration.

Allow yourself to feel excited about how the Universe will mirror back to you this wonderful state of being you've created in yourself. Let go of the envy and the belief: *I can't have what he has.* Start creating the abundance you deserve!

I have all that I could ever want. The Universe answers my joy with more joy, my abundance with more abundance. I am thrilled to see what the Universe is bringing me right now! I am open to all the fantastic, ingenious possibilities it has created for me.

As I look around me at all the wealth others enjoy, I feel tremendous excitement for them and for myself, because I know that I, too, have overflowing abundance. I live a life of luxury and opulence. I appreciate all the gifts the Universe gives to me and to everyone around me. It is fantastic to live in a world of wealth and riches!

I claim mine today. I deserve abundance. It is washing over me right now, filling me up with a sense of richness and gratitude.

I love my home . . . and all the wonderful gifts I have. . . . I am deeply grateful for all my wealth.

(**Note:** Everyone has different ideas about what they want. Don't hold back from wishing for what you most desire! Fill in this affirmation with specific images of what you desire if it helps you make your visualization of this luxury item more real for you, creating even stronger emotions of abundance, worthiness, and joy. When you do this, you'll find that whether you end up with a luxurious lake home with a patio where you entertain all your friends or simply a nice little home that suits your needs, you'll be pleased by how the Universe responded to your affirmation of what you're entitled to, and you'll be aware of how abundance manifests in all the areas of your life.)

Distinction #6

ALL THE RICHES YOU HAVEN'T RECOGNIZED OR CLAIMED IN THE PAST ARE STILL AVAILABLE TO YOU

At lunch the other day, Lisa, a client of mine, was complaining that she'd had a brilliant idea for an e-book, but someone else "stole" it and created an e-book on the same topic that wasn't as good as hers would have been. This other author had tremendous success with his project, and Lisa felt that he'd destroyed any possibility of hers becoming successful. "That e-book was my one big chance, and he blew it out of the water," she complained.

I said, "I think that was *a* big chance for you, not your 'one' big chance. If you came up with an idea as fabulous as that one, I'm sure you can come up with another."

Lisa looked at me skeptically, and I know what she was thinking: *There are no second chances!* Well, I don't believe that for a minute. I believe that if we open ourselves up to possibility and trust in the abundant, giving Universe, we'll have 2nd, 3rd, 4th, and 3,832nd chances! Look around and you'll see examples of people who reinvented their lives and went from rags to riches to rags to riches again.

"Maybe you weren't meant to write that particular e-book," I told Lisa. "Or maybe you *were* meant to write it, but in a different way, in your own voice—and it's going to be a much bigger success than you imagine. Or maybe it's not meant to be a book, but a business, a Website, or something else."

I told her about a friend of mine who had been approached by an editor to write a book on a particular topic. She'd created a book proposal that her editor loved, but his boss wouldn't let him buy the book, reasoning that my friend's take on the topic was far too lighthearted and fun, so it couldn't possibly sell in the marketplace. She went on to have a dozen publishers turn the book down before one signed it, and it went on to generate five sequels and sell a quarter-million copies in a half dozen languages. The book even inspired a television show based on it. Her "one big chance" seemed to have passed her by when that first publisher said no, but she chose to believe in second chances and an abundance of opportunities.

The Universe *wants* to give to you. The moment you begin to change your vibration to one of abundance, it will start sending you people, situations, and opportunities that reflect your inner state. You'll start to see possibilities for wealth creation, whether they're the exact ones you failed to notice previously or new ones.

It can be hard to let go of the feeling of *I blew it!* and watch as others enjoy the riches you passed by. Some friends of mine were trading stories once, and everyone had a family chronicle about "Uncle Theo," who sold that gorgeous brick home for a song without telling his brother, and nowadays it's worth a fortune . . . or of Great-Grandpa, who was too skittish to buy up beachfront property years ago and watched his best friend who did invest become a self-made millionaire, while *he* continued to have to work in the grocery store. As everyone told their family's tale, we had to laugh, because for all the lost chances, here we were, years later, enjoying tremendous abundance together. Would any of us really be all that much happier if that relative long ago wouldn't have made what seemed like a "disastrous" mistake at the time? I doubt it!

Over the years, I've heard many life coaches tell audiences that they've made a fortune, gone bankrupt, made a fortune, gone bankrupt again, and made another fortune . . . as if anyone who really wants to enjoy great wealth has to suffer ruin and huge ups and downs in their financial situation. I don't think that's true at all, but it *is* true, as I've said, that you have to be *willing* to give it all up. The key to letting go of the fear that you could lose all you've worked for is to accept that all the riches you haven't recognized or claimed in the past are still available to you. The door to abundance is never locked—it just sticks sometimes when you're not truly ready to receive wealth.

Sometimes the problem is that you're rushing about so quickly that you're missing opportunities. If you don't look closely or contemplate the possibilities, you might pass by a great chance for creating wealth, saying, "That will never work." I think that was the case with the editor who said my friend's book was too lighthearted to be successful! If you've missed an opportunity, don't kick yourself and create negative feelings. Trust that the next big break will come, and absorb the lesson of paying attention and allowing yourself to be open to the unexpected. Create positive feelings about what you learned from missing this particular chance. Then generate feelings of faith, trust, and creativity . . . and get ready for what the Universe is bringing you next.

Remember that even if you do lose everything, or a great opportunity slips away, there are more potential opportunities for wealth presenting themselves every single day. Maybe you'll wake up tomorrow and invent the equivalent of the pet rock—remember that fad from the 1970s? A fellow named Gary Dahl thought it would be funny to package an ordinary pebble and market it as the perfect pet: no need to feed it, walk it, or take it to the vet. Apparently, a lot of other people thought his idea was funny, and they bought enough pet rocks to make Gary Dahl a millionaire!

Let go of the past and all the negative feelings you've created about what might have been. Vibrate abundance and open yourself to the possibilities that will present themselves.

Every day new ideas and opportunities come to me. My inner wealth attracts increasing prosperity each day. My abundance is growing inside me and pulling in more and more riches, like a powerful magnet. I feel alive and excited by all the wealth that is in my life and all that is on its way to me!

I am deeply grateful for all the opportunities I have been given in my life. I have learned wonderful lessons that serve me well as I continue to expand upon all the riches I have. I have always been wealthy. I <u>will</u> always be wealthy! Wealth is mine!

Today I open my eyes to the abundance before me. I discover the value I have been overlooking, and I rejoice at finding it again. I am so exited to reclaim my wealth!

Distinction #7

INFINITE PATIENCE PRODUCES IMMEDIATE RESULTS

When you acknowledge and value the wealth you already have and create a feeling of abundance, you plant the seed for manifesting financial success in the physical world. The Universe pays attention to your vibration of abundance and responds in its own time. As Wayne Dyer has pointed out, there's nothing to be gained in standing over your garden with a stopwatch, fretting if a seedling doesn't peek through the earth immediately. If you become impatient and worried about whether your seedlings will grow and you pull up the shoots to check on them, you'll kill them. Panic, fear, lack, and other negative emotions change your polarity and cause you to repel, not attract, abundance and to uproot your plants before they can bear fruit.

One of my clients, Dave, was in sales, and whenever he started feeling scared that he wouldn't be able to meet his monthly sales quota, he would try too hard to sell his product to people. His too-strong approach backfired, because his potential customers sensed that he was motivated by his own need to make money, not by a genuine desire to help them meet *their* need to spend their money wisely on a product that had value for them.

I asked Dave to explore this fear, and he told me that he was very intimidated by his boss, who had threatened to lay off any salesperson who didn't meet his or her monthly quota. I said, "Do you think that maybe your boss, like you, is being driven by fear, and that's holding him back from getting the sales and the money that he would like to have flowing into the business?"

Dave agreed that this was probably the case. With my encouragement, he approached his boss to talk about how he might be able to fulfill his quota without having to be in a situation where he feared for his very job if he failed. As it turned out, Dave's boss was open to being creative and considering all the many options for increasing sales. Ultimately, Dave, his boss, and the other salespeople in the company came up with some clever ways to sell more of their product that they'd overlooked before because they were all so focused on achieving their specific goals by a specific time. As soon as the salespeople let go of their fears, they were able to use more effective, more relaxed selling techniques, and everyone's sales began to increase right away.

When bills start stacking up, it's important to resist negative emotions and to trust in the timing of the Universe. Some of my clients become very negative every tax season and actually experience a mild depression. One of them has said that she becomes depressed in the springtime on the anniversary of starting her business if she hasn't met her particular goals for the year because she feels disappointed in herself. What I always tell my clients is that the Universe has its own timing, and if you actively choose to create positive emotions about money—including the emotion of abundance—then it's only a matter of time before the physical world begins to reflect your inner state of wealth.

You switch into negative emotions the moment you begin worrying and thinking, *But when is the money coming?* As you change your vibration to one of lack and fear, you start repelling the riches that are on their way to you . . . so the trick to creating abundance is to stop wearing a watch! I don't mean that literally, of course. What I mean is that you need to have enough cash flow, credit, and good money-management skills to be able to keep your bills paid as you're waiting for the wealth to come in.

I have two clients who both work in an industry that's notoriously slow to pay its vendors. One has never accepted that this is how the industry works, and he constantly has cash-flow problems. He gets scared and angry and blames his customers for his situation. Year after year, he has struggled with this problem and still is plagued by it. The other client decided to accept that the industry is slow paying and made sure to have savings available to him, as well as credit so that he could borrow money whenever finances were tight.

With the security of knowing that he wasn't dependent on getting paid on time every time, he found it easier to create feelings of abundance, faith, and confidence, and this allowed him to find creative solutions to the problem of cash flow. He negotiated discounts for customers willing to pay quickly and raised his rates for those who were slow to do so, and he even dropped some of them. This was a little scary for him at first, but he created feelings of faith. Focused on the terrific value he brought to his customers, he learned to let go of that fear. He soon was attracting many new customers, and then it became very easy for him to maintain a cash cushion for himself—but now he rarely needs to use it, because he's attracting so much abundance.

Why can't we simply vibrate abundance and know without a doubt that we'll get the precise amount we need on the exact day we need it? Maybe it's because we're supposed to slow down once in a while and learn some lessons about abundance, creativity, and faith. The Universe is infinitely more inventive and clever in how it manifests abundance than we can imagine, but often we try to boss it around and force it to operate our way. We block it from operating the way *it* wants to because we think we know better.

Keep in mind that often you won't be able to perceive that the Universe is working with perfect timing until after the fact. Let's say that you miss out on buying the house you want because you can't get the financing due to an unfair mark on your credit that you didn't realize was there. Then you fix your credit problem and discover by talking to neighbors that the house you'd wanted wasn't such a bargain after all—and that a much better one has been placed on the market. You couldn't have foreseen that option coming down the road, but you could have trusted in the perfect timing of the Universe and been patient.

The more you start to have faith in the Universe, the more you'll see these sorts of miracles happen in your life and all around you, and the easier it will be to trust in the Universe the next time you're tempted to panic.

When you're experiencing a downturn in your fortunes and are starting to worry about the Universe's timing, imagine that you've just enrolled in a miniclass at the local community college called "Learning to Trust in the Universe while Being Open to Its Lessons." Imagine that you've paid your tuition to take this very valuable course that will benefit you for years to come. Think about how exciting it is to take a front-row seat and focus your attention on the professor, who's asking you provocative questions designed to foster your creativity and get you to replace your negative, destructive feelings with positive, constructive ones that will generate great abundance in your life.

Get ready for essay questions such as: "Why are you so uncomfortable with asking for the salary or fee you desire?" or "What valuables are you storing in a closet rather than using to create abundance for yourself? Why don't you take them out, dust them off, and exchange them for something else of value?" The professor in your mind will come up with all sorts of questions similar to these that will cause you to face the painful and unsettling negative feelings you've been denying and learn the lessons they have to teach you so that you can move past them.

Is your low self-esteem getting in your way? Do you discount your skills because you undervalue yourself? Is your fear of taking risks holding you back from manifesting abundance? Sometimes if you do foster abundance and trust in the timing of the Universe, it will surprise you by co-creating what you desire exactly when you think you need it.

Once, years ago, I took a big risk in moving into my dream home before I had the money to pay for it. The deal was that if I didn't come up with the down payment by December 1, I would have to move out and lose my deposit. I didn't know where the money was going to come from, but I vibrated faith, abundance, and gratitude as I enjoyed living in my lovely new home. My company decided to make their stock public, and as it turned out, I was able to cash out my shares exactly two days before I had to close on my house or move. What a close call!

Why was I able to attract the money I needed when I needed it? Because the Universe happened to be in sync with my timing, and I was continually creating positive feelings about myself and what I had that was of value. If the money hadn't manifested when I needed it, I would have trusted that the Universe had something better in mind for me.

Now, not everyone can tolerate the level of risk that I can, and it wasn't as if I didn't have options for housing my son and myself if the money didn't come through by December 1. I feel comfortable enough with money to risk it because I know there will always be more coming into my life. But too often people will put themselves in a situation where they're completely emotionally dependent on having the Universe provide exactly what they want when they want it because this gives them a false feeling of security. They'll tell themselves, *If I get that house [or that job, or at least $10,000] before the end of the quarter, I'll be okay.* Thinking in this way blocks the Universe from operating according to its timing and wisdom.

You're going to be okay no matter what happens, so be open to how the Universe responds to your vibration of abundance. Rather than attempting to micromanage the Universe, turn up the volume on positive feelings that allow you to be creative. My salesman client, Dave, and his boss explored new options for how to "sweeten the deal" and provide value for their customers—options they couldn't see when they were completely focused on achieving a specific dollar amount in sales by a certain date and were feeling fear and lack.

Once you've let go of your negative feelings and are experiencing trust in the Universe and its timing, you can leave the classroom and get moving. With enthusiasm and faith propelling you, you'll find it easier to take actions that will allow you to co-create with the Universe: You'll be able to pick up the phone and make a cold call, or do some research if you're not even sure where to start. You'll find the courage to go back to school, to admit you're lacking skills and start developing them or hire someone else who has them who can help you, or to consider a new career or a job change. Courage will come, and a wealth of possibilities will open up for you.

Even a strong magnet can't attract the smallest pin if that object is too far away. You have to either strengthen the magnet or move something—the pin or the magnet. If you vibrate positive emotions and act in accordance with your inner feelings of abundance, creativity, and trust, you'll be an even stronger money magnet. You'll find yourself moving closer to your goal and drawing in what you desire.

So if the roots of the seedling you've planted are still shallow, be patient. Leave no room for doubt and worry, because the Universe knows just when to make that seedling poke its head through the soil and when to allow the fruit ripen to perfection.

The Universe operates with perfect timing, and I completely trust in it. The wisdom of the Universe is infinite. I am working with the Universe and creating wealth right now. I am enjoying the many ways in which the Universe is manifesting riches for me!

Money is the rushing stream of water from the melting snow at the top of the mountain. It scrambles over rocks and soil and hurries to meet me. Wealth invigorates me as it flows into my life! I am excited to be rich!

As I practice supreme patience, I enjoy the riches that the Universe is manifesting in my life at this very moment. Thank you, Universe, for the tremendous abundance I have right now. I possess so much of value already! I have so many loving friends and family members in my life. I have an affectionate, caring partner who truly values me and reminds me of all my many gifts. I have an abundance of love and joy. I feel tremendous gratitude.

I have amazing talents and skills. I am greatly appreciated for the work I do. I have endless creativity, and I am always open to the many possibilities that are available to me at all times.

I am grateful for my excellent credit rating and my extremely high income that gives me tremendous wealth that flows forth from me and enriches others. I am grateful for my beautiful, opulent home and the bounty of healthful food I enjoy. I am so lucky to be in fantastic health. All my blessings attract more blessings. All my love attracts more love. All that I deserve—all that I desire—is flowing into my life at this very moment, and I receive it with deep gratitude and open arms.

(**Note:** Even if you don't have all that you desire, affirm that you do. Tailor these affirmations to meet your own wishes and truly believe what you're saying even if it doesn't match up with what's happening in the physical world right this moment. By creating the feelings you'd experience if you had each of these blessings in your life right now, you make yourself a magnet for all that you desire.)

Distinction #8

YOU DON'T HAVE TO KNOW HOW YOU'LL GET WHAT YOU WANT— YOU JUST HAVE TO DECIDE *WHAT* YOU WANT

Just as we frequently have difficulty trusting in the Universe's timing, we often find it a challenge to have faith in its decisions about the form our bounty should take. When we try to micromanage the Universe and define how it manifests abundance in our lives, we interfere with the wonderfully clever plan it has for us.

You don't have to know *how* you'll get what you want. Let the Universe attend to the details of that. All you have to do is know *what* you want and create the positive feelings that you'd experience if you already had what you wish for.

Maybe you're in debt or you need money in order to purchase something you desire—perhaps you want to send your child, or yourself, through school or you'd like to attract enough money to be able to travel. First, it's important to recognize that often you can get what you desire, even if it's something material, without having the money to pay for it. I know someone whose child received a full scholarship to college for an unusual sport that he happened to excel at. I'm acquainted with another person who temporarily traded homes with someone in Europe so that both could have a nice, affordable living space to enjoy while on vacation in a foreign country.

Don't assume that money is the sole solution to your problems and is the only form of abundance that you can exchange for what you desire. Be open to all the ingenious ways in which the Universe provides for you and look for the opportunities that will present themselves.

Often having just one amazing idea and being willing to work to bring it to the public has made someone wealthy. When you allow yourself to be creative and open to the Universe's way of responding to your vibration of abundance, you may come up with an idea that generates great wealth. Look at the bestseller lists and you'll see that many of the books were written by people who were living ordinary lives until something happened to them that they ended up writing about. You might have a story that has the potential to touch people's hearts and uplift them or to benefit them in some other way. You might have a clever idea that turns out to be a great solution to a vexing problem. Maybe you'll invent a product or service that millions of people will find useful.

Moreover, don't get stuck thinking that the only way in which you can get money is by earning it: exchanging a specific amount of work for a specific amount of money. You never know when a bonus, a windfall, or an unexpected source of cash will show up. Recently, I read in the newspaper that in Japan people are finding cash in their mailboxes and in public bathrooms. The police speculate that the money is coming from some people who, for whatever reason, want to share their wealth anonymously with strangers. Some of the stacks of cash discovered in bathrooms came with a note urging the finder to enjoy the money and put it toward a good purpose. In one apartment building, several unrelated people received the equivalent of $1,000 in cash in their mailbox, with no explanation.

What's interesting to me is that many of the recipients said they felt wary and uncomfortable about their find. Perhaps because they hadn't earned it, they didn't feel that they deserved to have it. Many of them called the police to report this "suspicious" money, and now the authorities have promised to hold it until someone claims it. Isn't it interesting that some people so strongly believe they have to earn any money they receive that they can't simply enjoy an unexpected windfall? What would you do if you found cash and couldn't locate the owner? How would you feel about the money?

I think most people would enjoy having the cash, but many might also feel guilty because they hadn't worked for it. Lottery winners and people who become wealthy very quickly often feel guilty because they now have a lot of money and those they love don't. They'll overspend or give away so much of the money that they're left with nothing. If they could feel entitled to this wonderful gift from the Universe, they might find positive ways to use their financial gain that would benefit them and others, and they'd be more likely to start learning how to manage the money because they'd feel worthy of having it and work with it.

I know several people who made a lot of money quickly and let it slip away somehow. They later realized that by not emotionally accepting that they had the money, they had actually repelled it with all their guilt and discomfort. Once they developed a positive attitude toward wealth, they were able to regain it, building upon the abundance they already had.

While you can choose to work for your money or exchange something of value for it (for example, selling possessions you own), you don't always have to do so. Money can come to you in many forms, often without your having to do anything to bring it in except to experience the emotion of abundance and change your vibration. When my clients are struggling to have faith that the Universe will provide, I remind them of all the many ways in which we can receive money unconditionally:

— **Gifts.** People love to give. When you receive their offerings with grace, you make them feel good because you allow them to experience the joy of being able to help another.

— **Bank errors.** When my friend was in her 20s and struggling financially, she received a gift of $200 from a relative who wanted her to be able to buy a television set. She put the money in her checking account, went to the store to look at televisions, then withdrew the money from an automatic teller machine and bought the TV she'd decided on. However, the withdrawal never showed up on her account. She went in and talked to the people at the bank, who told her that without her withdrawal slip, which she'd lost, there was nothing they could do to correct the error. She had to accept their unintended gift of an extra $200!

— **Money reclaimed through an audit.** A client of mine was widowed and, not having much savings or any life insurance to collect, didn't know how she'd pay her bills. She created feelings of faith and abundance and, to her great surprise, received a very large check in the mail from the government, which had done an audit and discovered that years before when her husband was receiving unemployment compensation, he'd been underpaid. The check was for the amount of the underpayment plus interest.

— **Lotteries, contests, and door prizes.** You have to play to win, but you don't necessarily have to spend a lot of money to have a chance of winning. Many lotteries are won by groups of people who invest a small amount for tickets, pool it, and share the wealth when they hit the jackpot. You can also win contests offered by manufacturers and advertisers, or a raffle. You never know! One of my clients learned of a contest sponsored by a butter company that offered a free trip for two to a tropical island to the person who could make the most cow-like mooing sound. Her husband, as it turned out, was an amazing mooer, and he mooed his way to winning! If you'd rather have cash than a prize, you can sell the prize to someone else.

— **Found money.** As those lucky people in Japan learned, you can find money on the street or just about anywhere. Whenever I see a penny on the ground, I pick it up, because while it may not have any buying power, it reminds me that the Universe is always giving to us.

— **Awards and rewards.** Without your knowing it, your friend might be writing in to a television show, telling them what a wonderful person you are and inspiring them to shower you with prizes and money. Or you might win an award that someone else nominated you for, and you might get cash along with it. A heroic young man who helped rescue children from a bridge collapse was reported to have recently dropped out of a trade school because he couldn't afford the tuition, and the school offered him a scholarship to reward him for what he'd done for those children and the community.

— **Forgotten financial holdings.** Newspapers often run listings of forgotten bank accounts or safe-deposit boxes.

— **Wills and death benefits.** This is a sad way to receive money, but you might inherit cash from a relative or a friend, or be a beneficiary on a life-insurance policy and not realize it.

— **Money for permission to use intellectual property you created or own.** If you created a book, song, or painting, someone might approach you with an offer to pay you for using it. Nonfiction works and even magazine articles have inspired movies, and recordings by mostly unknown musical artists have ended up in films, TV shows, and commercials. Then, too, you may have inherited the rights to an intellectual property created by one of your relatives many years ago that somebody wants to use.

— **Rental of your home or possessions.** Someone might want to rent your home, yard, store, boat, or other possessions to shoot photographs or films. The other day, I noticed film crews down the street and they told me they were filming a TV commercial in my neighbor's garage. I know someone who loans a field behind her house to her neighbor, who's a farmer, for planting, and in exchange he plows her driveway every morning all winter long. She used to have to pay a company a lot of money for this snow-removal service, and now that cash is freed up.

— **A reduction in expenses.** It seems that prices always go up, but once in a while bills are actually reduced, freeing you to spend your cash on something else. Then, too, you may realize that you no longer need to pay for a service you've been maintaining out of habit. One of my clients learned that the local government was offering no-interest loans for home owners looking to make their residences more energy efficient, and she was able to save a considerable amount of money on utility bills after taking advantage of the program and insulating her home.

— **Stock options.** Salary packages that include stocks can pay off big should the company become very successful.

Delight in the many ways the Universe comes up with to give you what you desire. Know what you want, and be open to how your call is answered.

Abundance is everywhere, and it is showing up in my life right now. The Universe provides money and riches to me in countless clever ways. I love to see all the many avenues the Universe creates in order to bring me even more wealth. I open my eyes to the opportunities the Universe creates for me and the possibilities it presents to me. Thank you, Universe, for all these wonderful opportunities and all this wonderful wealth flowing into my life.

All around and inside of me are resources I can use and exchange at any time. Within me is a gold mine. Everywhere I look, I see my resources, wealth, and prosperity. I have so much to give! I have so much to exchange! I love being rich!

Distinction #9

THE MORE VALUE YOU
GIVE UNCONDITIONALLY,
THE MORE YOU'LL HAVE

I recently returned from presenting a workshop in Cincinnati, and when I pulled up to the parking attendant's booth at the airport, I handed him my ticket and he flashed me a huge grin and said, "Hello! That'll be $30.50."

"$30.50?" I echoed, incredulous. "I was only here for 24 hours. I just want to pay for parking—I don't want to buy the place!"

He laughed and said, "Yep, it's $30.50 for 24 hours' parking. So how was your trip? Did you have a good time?"

I was still in a bit of shock at the price, but he was being so friendly that any temptation I had to become frustrated started to fade away. I chatted with him a little about my trip, asked him about his day, and paid my bill, feeling a lot better than I probably would have if he hadn't been so nice.

Now, some people might say that this gentleman had a right to be unhappy and cranky—after all, his job probably isn't always very pleasant. He has to deal with grouchy people who resent paying $30.50 for 24 hours' parking, he has to work in a closed space without much opportunity to move around or get visual stimulation, and he probably doesn't make all that much money. Yet this fellow was giving value unconditionally, without an obvious or immediate payback for doing so.

What he understood, which I try to help others understand, is that the more value you offer unconditionally, the more abundance you'll enjoy. Giving with strings attached creates feelings of fear *(What if I don't get a return on what I give?)* and lack *(I don't have enough to justify giving to others without a clear benefit to me).* Giving unconditionally creates feelings of abundance.

Giving value unconditionally means working with passion, enthusiasm, joy, humor, and a sense of worthiness. You value your time, money, resources, creativity, and hard work—as well as yourself—so you give not out of lack, but out of a desire to share your abundance.

It doesn't mean giving until you're burned-out and exhausted. If you're feeling that you've done far too much or are being taken advantage of, it's important to look at why you think that you must give more than you're comfortable giving. You may be doing so out of feelings of unworthiness, fear, and lack.

Experiencing negative emotions and giving too much will block the flow of abundance into your life and will instead present you with more opportunities to face those difficult feelings that you're avoiding, learn from them, and replace them with positive ones so that you achieve a balance of giving and receiving. These opportunities will probably look like problems— such as a boss who doesn't appreciate you or a relative who keeps begging you for money, spending it all, and asking you for more.

If you have the courage to face your difficult emotions of fear, lack, and unworthiness without judging yourself as bad or foolish, you can have the presence of mind to say, "These emotions aren't working for me. What positive feelings can I replace them with so that I can attract the abundance and joy I seek?" (In the material on Distinction #10, you'll find a chart listing specific negative emotions that can be replaced with specific positive ones that act as antidotes to the poison of negativity.) Create the positive emotions you deserve to feel, and watch as your tendency to give more than you feel comfortable giving disappears.

Although all of us should give unconditionally, everyone deserves to be compensated fairly for the value they bring to the world. Sometimes we take less than we deserve and trust that the Universe will find some way to compensate us for our unconditional generosity. We contribute money to a good cause, we offer free advice or services to someone who can't afford to pay, or we give from the heart to a stranger because we're feeling love and compassion. The Universe notices these actions—and the warm feelings that generate them—and responds by bringing love, value, and abundance into our lives in some way.

Recently, I received an e-mail from someone who seemed angry and unhappy, and she was basically saying, "You're so successful already. Why don't you just give away all your programs and books for free instead of trying to make more and more money?" From the tone of her e-mail, I suspect that she was feeling envious of me because she didn't realize that she can be just as affluent as I am. Perhaps she feels that if I have a lot and she has only a little, it must be because I'm taking something away from her or from a limited pool of abundance. What she doesn't understand is that she can have what I have, and she and I are both entitled to fair compensation for the value we give.

Rather than comparing our earnings with others' or trying to second-guess whether someone else is giving more than we are, we can adopt wealth consciousness: an understanding that riches flow in and out of all of us. This allows us to let go of fear and judgment and focus on maintaining our own balance of giving and receiving. We can be so quick to judge others, saying, "Look at her, wasting all that money on that luxury item!" No good can come of negatively judging others. So what if you have the money to shop at Neiman Marcus and you buy clothes at Kmart, or if someone else has a low income but chooses to splurge on a pair of shoes at Neiman Marcus? Every one of us is responsible for our own balance of giving and receiving and for offering value unconditionally, and it's not up to us to police anyone else. The more we practice wealth consciousness, the more we inspire others to do so.

My question to anyone who feels lack and envy is this:

"What can you do to foster a feeling of abundance and to give value unconditionally?"

People who feel wealthy and blessed and who bring value to their jobs regardless of their pay let the Universe know that they're ready to receive even more wealth. They may get a raise or an unexpected windfall, or they could attract the attention of someone who wants to hire them for a better job. As I drove away from that parking garage, I thought about how much value and enthusiasm that gentleman brings to his work if he is able to deal with grumpy customers all day long and by early evening still have joy to share with others. I thought, *I would like to hire that fellow!* I wouldn't be at all surprised if he gets a promotion, a raise, or a more lucrative position somewhere, and I imagine that he leads a rich and abundant life outside of his job.

When you give value unconditionally, you'll receive it in return—and the more you give, the more value and abundance you'll receive. People who offer the minimal amount at their job, always rushing out the door at exactly 5 P.M. and never showing any initiative, are missing the opportunity to create abundance or value and reap the benefits.

I have a client who oversees many employees. His company offers all workers free extra training, from in-house sessions on how to improve their skills to reimbursement for courses at local colleges. He tells me that once in a while an employee will come to him and say, "I've been working here for three years now, and I still haven't had a raise. I want one!"

He'll respond, "I understand how you feel. Tell me, what increased value are you bringing to the company? Have you gotten any more training and developed new skills? Have you shown initiative and offered a suggestion—or a solution to a problem—that has saved us money?"

Too often the employee will answer, "No, but I figure I should make more money because I've been here a long time."

My client will reply, "But I can hire someone tomorrow who will give me just as much value as you are giving, and they'll be happy with the entry-level salary. Why does working here for three years make you able to offer more value to this company than a newcomer can?" And usually the employee is silent.

There are many ways to offer value. My husband, son, and I live next to a golf course. At the end of the week, Michel will gather up all of the balls in our yard, put them in egg cartons, and sell them to golfers at a fraction of the cost of new ones. When he approaches a potential customer, he'll give them a free ball. Whether or not they decide to buy a dozen from him, this ball is theirs to keep. The golfers feel positive about him and are more inspired to buy a box from him, if not today, then sometime in the future.

You can offer value through creative ideas, suggestions for how to make your company work more efficiently, enthusiasm that inspires others, hard work, diligence and attention to detail, and going the extra mile in a crisis. Find the gold inside your Buddha and share it, knowing that the more you give, the more you'll receive.

If you can't muster the energy to provide more value, savor the prosperity that's already in your life and turn up the volume on your feelings of abundance, gratitude, and enthusiasm. It's great that you have work and skills and a way to support yourself! It's fantastic that you have an idea that you want to show the world! It's wonderful that you have the potential to share your abundance and build on it to manifest wealth! Work hard for the same reason children put all their energy into a game of tag—because it is, or should be, fun. If work isn't enjoyable, you're not connecting to a feeling of abundance.

Find the bounty that's in your life, and turn up the volume on your emotions of abundance, gratitude, and enthusiasm. You'll soon be at peace with your current situation and discovering ways to make it even better or to find more meaningful work. You'll create new opportunities and manifest wealth in all the areas of your life. That burned-out feeling will disappear.

When work, or the prospect of it, causes you to feel negative emotions, slow down and reconsider the course you're on. Do you need to widen your vision and alter your plan? Do you need to take some time off and reconnect with your feelings of abundance, passion, and creativity?

If you're thinking of finding different work, or you've been considering making a change for a long time but feel paralyzed and unsure of what to do next, start by creating positive feelings so that you can access your passion and creativity. You'll get clarity about what you want to do next and avoid making the kinds of mistakes we commit when we operate from negative feelings such as fear and lack. You won't jump from one unrewarding job to the next; instead, you'll find new, better opportunities opening up for you in response to the feelings of abundance, enthusiasm, and worthiness you've created. You'll recognize your beneficial purpose, value it, and attract more resources and wealth by giving unconditionally, letting your abundance flow into the Universe, and opening yourself to receive.

My work, ideas, skills, and talents are of great value. I have an infinite amount of abundance and worth. I have many blessings, and I love to share them with others. I have an extraordinary supply of love, and I give love unconditionally. I am a valuable contributor to the world, which appreciates all that I do and gives back to me continually. The Universe is bestowing great abundance on me, showering me with love and blessings.

I have so much to offer to the world, and I am giving it freely, from my heart. I give with passion, joy, and enthusiasm. I love sharing what I have. I am thrilled that I am inspiring others, and I rejoice at how they inspire me. I get excited thinking about all the many ways that value is flowing back into my life every minute of every day. I love receiving all the unexpected gifts that the Universe gives to me. I am so blessed!

Distinction #10

ALL OF YOUR POSITIVE EMOTIONS POSITIVELY INCREASE THE FLOW OF ABUNDANCE TO YOU

In my book *Your Destiny Switch,* I explain that emotions are like colors of the rainbow, and they all come from the same source: the white light of love. Love is the most powerful emotion of all because it contains all the positive emotions, including abundance, which is the opposite of lack. Love is so powerful that it's dazzling!

Love truly conquers all. It provides illumination that dispels the dark emotions and allows us to have insight into our thoughts, feelings, and actions so that we can transform them into more loving ones. We can dissolve the emotion of lack and instead feel abundance. We can replace any negative feeling with its opposite, positive one:

Replace this negative emotion . . .   . . . with this positive emotion

Lack	Abundance
Fear	Faith
Depression	Bliss
Hate	Love
Insecurity	Confidence
Rage	Calm
Loneliness	Harmony
Emptiness	Wonder/Creativity
Discouragement	Enthusiasm
Worthlessness	Worthiness

When you replace a negative emotion with a positive one, it's as if you push up a dimmer switch that increases the light in the room:

Abundance

Lack

Turn up the "volume" on your abundance and you'll stop experiencing lack. Turn it up on faith and you'll stop experiencing fear.

Now, imagine that all the emotional pairs of opposites are dimmer switches on a long switchboard, and that there's a string connecting all the levers.

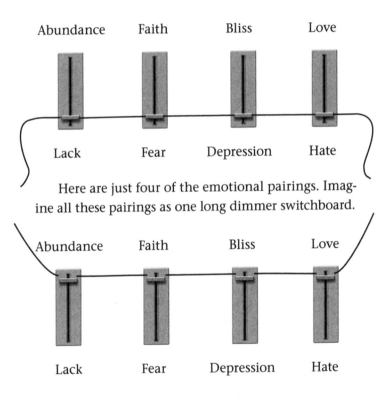

Here are just four of the emotional pairings. Imagine all these pairings as one long dimmer switchboard.

Pull the thread upward and all the levers will rise.

Raising any lever is like lifting the string at both ends: You pull all the levers upward. When you create just one positive emotion, you replace all your negative feelings with more positive ones.

As you've learned so far in this book, emotions such as lack, fear, and envy actually repel wealth, while the positive emotion of abundance attracts it. Create a positive emotion, such as worthiness, and you'll automatically increase your feeling of abundance—and you'll attract more wealth. You'll also draw to you people and situations that are in sync with your other positive emotions. The more love you feel, the more of it you'll have in your life. The more joyful you are, the more you'll find that joyous situations and people are appearing in your life. I love that there are so many ways to create abundance through the enormous power of positive emotions!

That said, there are specific emotions that are especially helpful in increasing your riches. One, of course, is a feeling of abundance. Many people were taught that if you feel abundant, you'll become arrogant instead of humble, but this isn't possible. Positive feelings never increase negative ones; they can only increase other positive emotions. If you want to attract wealth into your life, it's important to truly experience a sense of abundance every day.

Abundance includes the feelings of gratitude and expansiveness. When you feel full of riches, you automatically are grateful for them and want to share them with others so that they, too, can enjoy the wonderful feelings you're experiencing. One terrific way to create a feeling of gratitude is to keep a gratitude journal. Each night, write down a list of all the wonderful things that happened to you that day and all the blessings in your life that you have right now. Be thankful for your health, loved ones, home, food, and clothing. Be grateful for your wealth, your opportunities, and your work. Express appreciation for your education and your wisdom, your skills and your talents, and all the unique qualities that make you the person you are. Be grateful for all the love and abundance in your life and for everything that makes you laugh or feel wonder— anything that creates a positive feeling in you.

Today, for instance, I'm grateful for the pool in my backyard, the cool water that is just the perfect refreshing temperature, the warm sunshine, the time to enjoy a swim, and Michel and Denis, who are able to enjoy the pool along with me. In fact, every day I take the time to list or say aloud all that I'm grateful for. Every day, I'm thankful for that pool. On rainy days when I can't use it, I'm thankful for the beautiful sound of the rain tapping against my roof, and I'm grateful for a good, solid roof over my head, and—more than that—for a home to shelter me that's beautiful and big. On snowy days, I'm grateful for my snowplow service, my strong teenage son who can shovel the walkway, and the beauty of the falling snowflakes.

Every day, as you cultivate gratitude, you generate all the other positive emotions, making yourself more of a magnet for wealth, love, beauty, and everything else you desire.

Another very helpful emotion for creating abundance is faith, which dissolves fear. Fear paralyzes us and makes us stop believing that the Universe has unlimited abundance and is always giving. Fear distorts our thoughts, causing us to overlook the many blessings in our lives and all the evidence that the Universe is continually giving to us and everyone else. Faith, the belief in things unseen, allows us to trust that the Universe is providing, even if our situation in the physical world isn't quite in sync yet with our newly created emotions of trust and abundance.

Remember that the Universe works on its own timetable, according to its own wisdom and plan. As soon as you make a change within, it will begin to respond to that change by manifesting situations and people that are in sync with your new inner state, but those manifestations—the job opportunity, the cash you need to pay your bills, and so on—might not appear instantaneously.

Maybe your fortunes are rapidly being depleted—your business is going under, your house is being foreclosed upon, you're being audited or are facing an expensive lawsuit, or some other situation is causing you to get into debt. When you've been experiencing negative emotions—whether it's lack, fear, low self-worth, or any other—you can switch them quickly, but you must give the Universe time to respond with changes in the physical world. You may even find that your fortunes continue their downward momentum for a while, making it harder to have faith and not to panic. When this is the case, it's extremely important to maintain faith and a feeling of abundance.

When you do so, you'll also start feeling another crucial emotion in wealth creation: creativity. People often don't think of creativity as an emotion, but that's what it is—it's a feeling of openness or curiosity that helps you to see all the possibilities you overlook when you're experiencing negative emotions or indifference. Creativity compels you to say, "Isn't that curious?" and to wonder about the possibilities before you. It turns you into an explorer as new ideas start to appear and new paths begin to reveal themselves.

Remember Dave, the salesman who was frozen in fear at the thought of not making his monthly quota? Abundance, faith, and creativity allowed him to trust that he could find new ways to use his talents and skills to attract more clients and sales. Curiosity allowed him to observe his customers' subtle signals about how they were feeling toward his product line. Creativity helped him figure out ways to match up his products with their needs.

Explore the palette of positive emotions available to you. Each is a key to creating abundance!

Abundance is mine. I am overflowing with riches. I am deeply grateful for the blessings in my life, which are . . .

(**Note:** When you recite this affirmation, list your current blessings as well as those you'd like to have. Be as specific as you need to be in order to create positive feelings inside yourself.)

*I have the power to choose positivity. In this moment,
I opt to feel faith. I trust in myself, in the people around
me, and in humanity. I have faith in the Universe and its
infinite wisdom. Today, I have all that I need, and I know
that I always will. I know that I can trust myself and
that there are other people I can trust. I know that I can
always trust the Universe, which has an unlimited supply
of abundance and is always giving. It is giving to me right
now! At this moment, wealth is manifesting before my eyes.*

*I am a creative person. My life is a work of art. I approach
it with creativity and curiosity. I am open to new ideas,
people, and situations. I delight in discovering possibilities.*

Distinction #11

DWELLING IN NEGATIVE EMOTIONS
SLOWS THE FLOW OF ABUNDANCE

Positive emotions increase and attract abundance, so the more positive we are, the more easily we pull in riches, money, opportunities, and situations that match up with our feeling of being tremendously wealthy. Negative emotions, in contrast, have the power to decrease and repel abundance. Just as experiencing any positive emotion will turn up the volume on all the other positive emotions, experiencing any unpleasant emotion will result in your feeling many additional negative ones (remember that thread connecting all the emotion levers on your switchboard?).

The more negative your emotional state, the more you'll repel the abundance you deserve. Imagine that the flow of abundance is a creek filled with sparkling, clear water flowing toward you. Its current easily carries the water forward. Experiencing anger, sadness, fear, or jealousy is like dropping a big boulder into that creek. It continues to flow toward you, but its path has narrowed, and some of the water may be directed elsewhere or be slowed down as it makes its way toward you. Dwelling in a continual state of negative emotions is like dropping dozens of boulders into the creek, completely blocking the flow and forcing the fertile waters to move in another direction, away from where you are downstream.

Negative emotions aren't just unpleasant; they're actually very destructive. They can affect your health, causing illness and making you age prematurely by putting stress on all of your body's systems. They can be so powerful that they drag you down into a paralyzing depression, blocking your flow of abundance completely. This is why it's crucial to replace negative emotions with positive ones.

However, negative emotions do have some value: They serve to wake you up to harmful thoughts and behaviors that you need to be conscious of so that you can deliberately choose to replace them with positive beliefs and actions. Once you've begun the habit of exploring your negative emotions and their origins, you'll find that you've developed the habit of self-insight. You'll have learned to tolerate the discomfort of feeling sadness, anger, jealousy, fear, or unworthiness and to explore what the emotion teaches you. You'll probably discover that the same hidden, destructive beliefs keep cropping up in your mind again and again, creating those dark emotions. That's why I always say it's important not to be afraid of or ashamed of your negative emotions. They're a natural part of life that can't be avoided altogether, and they can be very beneficial when used as tools for discovery and healing. It's only when you begin to dwell in negative emotion that you start slowing the flow of abundance to the point where it's a mere trickle.

To break out of a habit of dwelling in negative emotions, you must become aware of what you're doing to foster them. Let's say that you discover, as I did once many years ago, that your mind keeps clinging to the belief: *I'm unworthy of love, joy, and prosperity.* Obviously, this thought creates feelings of unworthiness, sadness, and lack. And I'm sure that if others expressed to you that impression of themselves, you'd quickly reassure them that it's a false, ugly, and destructive belief and urge them to discard the thought immediately. But it's hard to let go of these beliefs if they're deeply ingrained in you. The way to get rid of them is to recognize how distorted and damaging they are and *consciously* choose to replace them every single time you discover them inside you. When you say, "Wait a minute, I don't believe that anymore!" you actually stop the automatic downward movement of the levers on your emotional dimmer switches. You stop creating negative emotions.

A little bit of poison can kill, and a little bit of destructive emotions or beliefs can crush your spirit and cause you to start to feel hopeless and powerless. Any and all of the positive emotions serve as potent antidotes to the poison of negative emotions. Construct positive beliefs to replace your negative ones and affirm them, creating positive emotions as you do so. Say out loud, with great feeling: "I am a lovable, valuable person with unique gifts to share with the world." Every day, affirm all your wonderful qualities.

Maybe your negative emotions are based in negative beliefs not about yourself, but about money and prosperity. You've probably heard the sayings "Money is the root of all evil" and "It's easier for a camel to go through the eye of a needle than for a rich man to get into heaven." Maybe you were taught to distrust wealthy people and to feel guilty about having "too much money" (because, of course, if you believe that there isn't enough abundance to go around, you have to be sure that you only enjoy your fair share of it and no more). But these beliefs are misunderstandings of great truths.

The Bible actually says: "The *love of* money is a root of all kinds of evil." It's referring to an attachment to achieving wealth in a very specific form, and being miserly and greedy instead of expansive, loving, and generous. The verse about the camel refers to a pack animal, loaded down with all the possessions and wealth it feels it has to hold on to. When we're attached to money, not seeing it as simply one form of wealth and sharing it generously with the world, we're like that camel, clinging to our possessions and wealth and afraid of losing them. Our fear and attachments block us from feeling happy and contented.

People who have a lot of money but are continually experiencing emotions of fear and lack *(What if I lose it all? What if there isn't enough of it for me tomorrow?)* or anger and resentment *(I deserve to have all this money and not share it or give it to anyone else, because I've suffered!)* eventually drive away abundance. They may be able to maintain a lot of money for a long time, but the other forms of abundance will dry up for them. They'll be miserly with love, compassion, kindness, and understanding, which is no way to live.

In contrast, people who don't have much money but who are regularly experiencing positive emotions become money magnets and wealthy in many different ways. They may not even desire a lot of riches because they prefer abundance in other forms. There's nothing wrong with wanting a yacht, and there's nothing wrong with simply wanting plenty of time to sit on the dock enjoying the sunset and watching other people's yachts pass by in front of you. What's most important isn't the kind of abundance you have or desire, but that you have positive feelings about wealth in all its forms.

Recently, a client of mine came to the conclusion that she could either rent a home in the neighborhood where she wanted to live or buy a home in another community where housing prices and taxes are lower. She feels a tremendous sense of abundance as she looks at her beautiful, large apartment; the wonderful public school in the neighborhood that she's able to send her children to; and the rich network of friends and family she has in her community. Leaving that all behind to gain equity in a house elsewhere doesn't appeal to her. She has abundance in her life, and as long as she experiences it and feels the power of that emotion, she'll continue to attract riches. Maybe she'll receive that wealth in a form that will allow her to purchase a home in her current neighborhood, and maybe she won't—but even if she doesn't, her abundance will serve her and make it easier for her to feel happiness.

My client is even able to feel abundance despite having a significant debt, and she believes that by continuing to vibrate gratitude and wealth, she'll eventually attract enough money to pay it off. She makes a point of not feeling negative about the money she owes, and instead feels positive about creating wealth so that she can continue to chip away at that debt.

Negative feelings often surround debt, causing it in the first place and then worsening it. Very often people overspend out of a feeling of lack, fear, or unworthiness. When they see that they've accrued debt, those negative feelings increase and they spend even more. People often avoid facing up to and addressing their debts because they don't want to feel the guilt, shame, or fear they would experience if they thought about how much they're in the hole. In fact, creditors capitalize on these fears. Although they know that their power to force someone to pay off their debt immediately is extremely limited, they recognize that most people don't know that and won't research their rights—they'll just get scared and follow the creditors' lead, feeling pressured into paying more than they can handle.

Many of my clients come to me seeking advice on how to rid themselves of debt, and I tell them that the most important thing to know is that you must let go of judgments and negative emotions about it. Only then can you create the positive emotions that will bring you the courage that will allow you to tolerate your negative feelings as you explore why you got into debt. You can learn the lessons of your debt and then move on to create wealth, deal with what you owe, and put yourself back into the black instead of the red.

The steps for getting out of debt are:

1. Simply observe your negative emotions. You might feel guilty for overspending, or angry because you made a business decision that turned out badly for you. When you think about your debt, identify the negative emotions that surface and that are connected to your dark thoughts. If you're thinking, *I shouldn't have listened to my friend about that investment!* or *What will I do when that credit card bill comes in and I can't afford the minimum payment?* identify the negative feelings those thoughts are creating and reinforcing.

2. Let go of judgment. The problem with judgment is that it creates destructive, negative emotions. Don't dismiss yourself as irresponsible or foolish. Don't cast judgments on other people: the individual you loaned money to who didn't give it back, the person who gave you bad advice, the customer who didn't pay his bill, and so on. It's not helpful to judge yourself or anyone else negatively. If you did something you shouldn't have, you'll deal with that in a moment. For now, move on to the next step. . . .

3. Learn from your negative emotions and your experiences. Your negative feelings may have been so deeply buried that you didn't recognize them until just now. Often they're repressed because they're so painful to experience. Allow yourself to process them, and have faith that you'll move through them and even benefit from them, because they have a lot to teach you. My guess is that at the root of your imbalance between spending and income are negative feelings such as lack, anger, unworthiness, or fear.

You may have thought that these feelings could empower you in some way; for instance, many people mistakenly believe that anger makes them strong and able to fight for what they need and desire. There's no need to fight to get what you want, and anger doesn't strengthen you—it weakens you. Spending out of anger—to get back at a spouse or to rebel against your parents—simply hurts you. By exploring your negative emotions, you'll start to see how they didn't create the feelings of abundance, love, and worthiness that you believed they could stir in you. You'll start to see the behavior patterns you've been ignoring, patterns that you can change once you're aware of them.

4. Decide to switch from negative emotions into positive ones. Choose a positive emotion to replace your negative one, and act now to create it. Switching emotions is as easy as flipping on a light. I know that it may not seem that way, but there are many ways to switch your feelings almost instantaneously. You can say, "I've had enough of that feeling!" or walk out of the room, take a deep breath, and tell yourself, *This anger isn't working for me. What positive emotion would I like to feel?* Then you can start remembering an instance when you felt a positive emotion or imagining a scenario in which you would feel it. If you're trying to create abundance, remember that time when you were enjoying a delicious meal with friends and delighting in the companionship and good food, or imagine yourself living in splendor and writing a huge check to charity.

Let your imagination run free and see what images of abundance come up for you. As the scene plays in your mind, allow your feeling of abundance to rise up inside you. Don't let creditors influence you to feel fearful or guilty.

5. Act in accordance with your new, positive feelings. Transform what you have of value into payment for your debt. Work hard, come up with new ideas for generating money, and look for opportunities to create more wealth. Remember, too, that when you give value unconditionally, you'll increase your wealth—don't get attached to how much money you want to create, and when. Know your rights. Look into loans, debt consolidation, and credit-management services, which are low cost or even, in some cases, free. Learn the lessons of your debt and accept the consequences: Get a second job, sell your possessions, move into a smaller home, or do whatever it is you have to do to pay off what you owe and increase your wealth—but remember that whatever you do, it's important to create positive emotions about bringing wealth into your life. Enjoy how exciting it is to make payments on your debt and to see it being whittled down.

6. Ask for help if you so choose. If you'd like to approach someone to help you with your debt, be aware of the specifics of your financial situation and begin by explaining just how you got into debt, what you've learned from the experience, and how you've changed your spending habits. Remember that there's no value in creating negative feelings about owing money. Take responsibility for it and let the other person know what you'd like him or her to do for you: pay off the debt, loan you money, guide you in finding ways to increase your income and get out of the red, cosign a loan, and so forth.

Be open to, and grateful for, whatever assistance they can give you. If other people can't offer you anything of value—not even understanding and encouragement—and instead are angry, judgmental, or resentful, accept that they have chosen to feel negative about your request and don't respond by creating negative feelings.

7. Make amends, with love. If you treated someone unjustly during the creation of the debt—perhaps you borrowed a lot of money you can't pay back as you promised, or you avoided someone after that person gave you a loan because you felt guilty—create a feeling of love for yourself and anyone you wronged. When you feel loving toward yourself and others, you'll find the courage to admit to them that you did something they found hurtful. You'll be brave enough to say, "What can I do to make it up to you?"—and you'll make amends. If you can't make amends to the one you harmed because the person feels so hurt that he or she won't forgive you, bless that individual, express your love and gratitude to him or her, and make a point of giving of value, unconditionally, to the world.

Many people find it challenging to let go of negative emotions surrounding debt, such as guilt or fear, but it doesn't have to be a difficult task. If you face your situation and find out what your options are, it will be even easier to replace those negative emotions with positive ones. Positive actions will enhance your positive thoughts and feelings. Talk to a credit counselor, negotiate a payoff and accept that you have a black mark on your credit rating for now, and pay your friend back $10 a month if that's all you can afford to put toward a large, outstanding loan. If you want to ask someone for financial assistance, be respectful by taking responsibility for your money situation and changing your behavior so that you can improve it.

Remember that wealth is a force. If you're headed in the right direction, that force will help you get out of debt. If you're still engaging in the same behaviors that led to the debt, money won't help you in any lasting way. Change internally before asking others to come to your aid, and be forthright and honest with them about your finances. Remember that people who care about you do want to help, but they want to be sure that they're not simply enabling you to continue with the same old patterns of thinking, feeling, and behaving that haven't been working.

Do what has to be done to create positive emotions about attracting wealth and changing your financial situation. Taking positive action will help you feel more positive about yourself.

Whatever you do, *never be ashamed of your debt.* Shame is a destructive emotion that will ultimately block your ability to attract wealth and abundance. You may have overspent because of negative feelings and not realized it, and you aren't going to do that anymore. Now that you know you've been experiencing destructive emotions, you can replace them and your spending behaviors will change. Also, you might have gotten into debt because you were overburdened by caring for a loved one (a new baby, an ill spouse, or an elderly parent who is becoming more frail) and couldn't put your energy into generating income.

If you gave value unconditionally, don't lose faith that the Universe will respond with abundance. Notice the abundance you have already: love, a close relationship with your spouse, a sense of accomplishment, new skills, and so on. Wealth in the form of money will come along, too. Be certain that you're ready for it, and be patient. Whenever negative feelings come up, keep replacing them with positive ones and don't dwell in them.

There are many specific techniques for switching emotions that I discuss in *Your Destiny Switch,* but whichever ones you decide on, make a habit of using them. Work the program described in the Introduction of this book.

This investment of just a few minutes in the morning is like consuming an emotional power drink that fuels me. In the middle of the day, reciting my affirmations keeps me aware of what my goals are and reinvigorates me, and at night, it helps me end my day on a positive note, and I sleep well. Commit to the 21 Distinctions of Wealth program and see how effective it is!

*I love and accept myself and the choices I have made.
I have learned great lessons, and I am continuing to learn
even more valuable lessons. I am growing every day,
becoming wiser and wiser. I am in control of my finances,
and I feel great about the flow of wealth.*

*My financial situation is healthy and positive! I am
creating wealth. I am manifesting riches! I am in charge of
my spending, and I use my abundance wisely. I give value,
unconditionally, and I receive it, unconditionally.*

*I trust in the Universe and its wisdom. I have faith that it
is moving abundance around and providing all the wealth
I need, when I need it. I open my heart and receive the
wisdom and riches the Universe wants to share with me.
I open my arms and receive the abundance it is bestowing
on me. I am so grateful for the flow of money in my life.*

(**Note:** When you are affirming your abundance,
don't use the word *debt* or the term *getting out of debt*.
Debt carries a vibration of lack and creates that emotion.
Instead, affirm all that you have. Recognize the lessons
you've learned as a result of incurring debt and facing

the hidden emotions and beliefs you held that caused you to get into it. Be grateful for these lessons. And when you recite the affirmation "I open my arms and receive the abundance . . ." you may want to spread your arms wide in order to help you truly feel receptive to abundance.)

Distinction #12

YOUR DESIRE TO HELP ANOTHER BECOME ABUNDANT CREATES MORE ABUNDANCE FOR YOU

I have a passion for helping others discover, nurture, and grow their abundance. My passion inspires me to work hard and to be creative in finding ways to share my knowledge with others. Every time I get an e-mail from someone thanking me for my words of advice and inspiration, I feel rich!

However, in following my passion, I sometimes do experience challenges. For instance, I'm not crazy about public speaking, but I feel I need to do it in order to help others benefit from my abundance of knowledge about manifesting what they desire. I get very nervous whenever I have to address a large group, and in the past I often avoided it. Yet, I want to help others create abundance in their lives so that they can share my joy and sense of prosperity, and lecturing allows me to meet this goal. So, while I still dread getting up onstage, I force myself to do it. I replace my feelings of fear with ones of joy as I think about how my speech might help others change their lives for the better. Afterward, I'm always glad that I met the challenge because, inevitably, someone in the audience will come up to me and tell me that my speech made a positive impact.

All of us have something of value to share with others, and we each have different challenges. You may love public speaking and be great at it but need to learn how to be a better listener. It may be a challenge for you not to tell others what to do and instead encourage them to develop their own insights and wisdom so that they can find their own solutions to problems.

Then, too, when you share your abundance, people don't always appreciate what you're offering. Trust that there are those who will value what you have to give and will use it to manifest even more value in their own lives. If others don't appreciate your gifts, bless them and don't create negative feelings about them. Don't feel that you have to win their approval by giving and giving. Let them discover the value of abundance on their own. By desiring to help them, you create a feeling of generosity and enthusiasm in yourself. These positive emotions make it easier for you to let go of negative thoughts and feelings, to feel generous, and to vibrate and attract abundance. Remember that the Universe blesses us with prosperity so that we can invest it back into the world and create even more riches for everyone to enjoy.

There are many forms of wealth and many ways to share it. Simply smiling at another person can be a tremendously powerful act of giving. A friend of mine enjoys smiling sympathetically at moms and dads whose toddler is crying and carrying on in public, and saying, "Somebody needs a nap!" The parents inevitably drop their embarrassment and frustration and visibly lighten up when she makes this comment. My friend's abundance of kindness and sympathy helps create the same feelings in others.

Many published authors begin with an abundance of passion for their subject, pouring it into a blog, a Website, or an organization. They share their wisdom and compassion with others through the media, making a video for YouTube, writing a letter to the newspaper, or speaking around the country and leading workshops. Their goal is simply to "get the word out," but their hard work and enthusiasm attracts the attention of a literary agent or publisher, and the next thing you know, they have a book deal and are on national television talking about their passion. It's the people looking for a "quick buck" who peter out long before they get to the point of writing a book, because they just don't have an abundance of passion for their subject.

Focus on the abundance you have—love, wisdom, interest in a subject, compassion, or humor—and nurture it so that you can share it with the world. Find a way to make the world better simply because you can, not because you're expecting a specific payoff. I'm glad that I make money from my work, but what really gives me a thrill is when I open an e-mail from someone thanking me for writing my books and giving my workshops, saying that I helped them. Knowing that I've aided one other person gives me a deep sense of joy and makes me feel grateful for my gifts and for all the opportunities I have for sharing them. I feel thankful for all those who help me—from my editor to my assistant to my son and husband, who love and support me. I feel a connection to others and recognize that the more abundance I create for myself, the more it flows out to others and makes them rich as well.

Feel the full force of the powerful emotion called "abundance." Let the Universe respond to your inner gold mine in its own way, as it surely will, and be thrilled that your abundance can uplift others and help them create it, too.

Give unconditionally, serve others, and don't put a limit on the riches you receive from the Universe in response to your giving. Trust that you can handle all that the Universe has in store for you, and that you can manage your wealth with grace and beauty. Hold on to your faith that it will flow through you to others just as it's supposed to. I know that you're going to make a big difference in the world in your own way!

I am grateful for all the special gifts that make me who I am. I love myself. I am rich, and I cherish being generous. I am thrilled to watch others experience love and abundance. It is thrilling to nurture others. I love to inspire people.

My light inspires others. My abundance flows into the lives of those around me, and they share my joy as we experience wealth together. I savor each moment that I have the power to influence another to join me in feeling rich and teeming with possibilities.

Distinction #13

Your Gratitude and Appreciation for Your Own and Others' Abundance Causes You to Become Even More Abundant

Gratitude is a wonderfully powerful emotion. Appreciation is the positive attitude or mind-set that we have when we're experiencing gratitude and acknowledging all the abundance in our lives. The heart's feeling (gratitude) and the mind's perception (appreciation) come together to create in us an emotional and mental state of abundance. Then the Universe responds to our vibration, mirroring it back to us by bringing us situations and people that reflect our inner state of wealth and plenty.

To create gratitude and appreciation, you may have to adjust your way of thinking. Thoughts influence our feelings, and often we'll bury negative beliefs in our subconscious because they create uncomfortable emotions. By recognizing these beliefs and replacing them with more uplifting thoughts, we make it easier to experience positive feelings.

Then, too, it's very easy to fall into a pattern of focusing on the negative and seeing the glass as half-empty, your bank account balance as "not enough," your partner as lacking, and so on. If you make a point of recognizing and acknowledging the positive aspects of your life, you'll be appreciative. You'll not only feel gratitude and have a great attitude, you'll actually *appreciate,* or nurture, your feeling of having been blessed, which will increase your ability to draw in and maintain wealth.

Every day, you can choose to create feelings of wonder, excitement, abundance, and gratitude. When you get up in the morning, take a moment to say a prayer of gratitude that you're waking to a day filled with possibilities and that you have the health to enjoy it and the freedom to choose your emotions regardless of what happens. Savor your breakfast. Say a prayer of thanks for your food, and imagine that every person in the world is sitting down to a nice, inviting breakfast just as you're doing. While you visualize millions of people enjoying their morning meal, feel abundance and gratitude. Imagine your wonderful feeling of plenty carrying across the world and entering the heart of every person on the planet. Your mind may try to protest, saying, *But there are people starving in the world!* That's true today, but it doesn't have to be true tomorrow. When you feel abundance and are inspired to share it with others, you lift others up to your level of abundance. It all starts with feeling gratitude and plenitude, and with the desire to share those feelings.

Throughout the day, stop yourself again and again as you go about your usual business and create a sense of gratitude that you envision spreading into the hearts of people everywhere. Feel thankfulness for your clothes as you're getting dressed. Be grateful for those people who grew and harvested the cotton that went into the material of your clothes, as well as those who diligently sewed them, packed them, shipped them, and sold them. Feel thankful for your car, your children, and the wonderful neighborhood and schools they enjoy as you drive them around. Be thankful for your dog as you go for a walk, or your cats as you feed them. At every opportunity, all day long, create feelings of abundance and wonder for what you have. Be in awe of your good fortune.

Make a point of sharing your own abundance with others so that you may inspire them to feel abundant, too. Even if you only have a cramped studio apartment, a box of crackers, and some apples to serve as refreshments, invite people over. Let them share in your bounty. Allow them to enjoy your loving home and to feel the energy radiating from your smile. Be generous with your time, money, love, and encouragement. Inspire them to laugh as you tell them a joke and share your sense of humor. Being able to share what you have will make you feel more abundant.

In his book *Man's Search for Meaning,* Viktor Frankl recalled how when he was imprisoned in German concentration camps in World War II, some of his fellow prisoners, who were starving and forced to do manual labor, would give away their last precious scrap of bread and offer comfort to others. These people understood that no one had the power to take away their freedom to choose to be positive and express compassion, and they decided that holding on to their humanity was absolutely crucial for their well-being. Frankl believed that positive feelings and attitudes were what kept men and women alive in the grimmest conditions. We can all learn about the value of sharing our own abundance with others from this example.

So replace any feelings of scarcity with ones of abundance, and share your resources with those around you. Offer whatever you can, whether it's money, assistance, love, compassion, or practical help.

Be sure that you're open to what other people's needs are, rather than imposing your own ideas on them. Ask them, "What can I do to help you?" Then give from the heart and enjoy the feeling of abundance you experience as a result.

You can also create the powerful feelings of gratitude and abundance by being thankful for others' abundance. If you resist the tendency to be envious or to feel competitive with those who are experiencing wealth and riches, you can truly enjoy their success and cultivate your own at the same time.

In our culture, we're rarely encouraged to appreciate others' wealth and abundance. Mostly we're encouraged to do the opposite. There are many Websites, TV shows, and tabloids devoted to criticizing and ridiculing successful people, and it's become commonplace to cast suspicions on anyone who is wealthy, famous, or powerful. Every time we engage in negative beliefs about wealth and create feelings of competitiveness and jealousy, we miss an opportunity to create feelings of gratitude and abundance.

Recently, Denis, Michel, and I were visiting a resort area in the U.S. where many wealthy people have second homes and enjoy owning and driving restored vintage cars and other rare, expensive vehicles. We had great fun looking at all of these marvelous cars, pointing, smiling, waving, and tooting our own horn and giving the thumbs-up to those riding in a bright blue 1920s-style roadster with canary-yellow wheel covers, a two-toned '50s sedan, or a bold red '60s convertible with leather interior. The drivers and their riders would inevitably smile and wave back. We were vicariously enjoying their abundance and creating a sense of gratitude and thankfulness. After all, it was as if we'd gotten free tickets to a car show! What a delightful surprise to see so many curious vehicles— and the drivers were clearly enjoying themselves as they shared their abundance with us and were taking great pleasure in our admiration of their cars. It was a wonderful day, and we had fun keeping an eye out for the next unusual vehicle.

When we appreciate others' value and abundance, we help them to feel abundance instead of lack and to give from generosity and the desire to share their wealth rather than from any need to ease their feelings of inadequacy, powerlessness, or unworthiness. We've all experienced people who pressure us to take their advice or adopt their way of thinking. This can be quite a challenge, especially if they're forceful and we're feeling insecure. When this happens, create feelings of faith, creativity, and abundance. Appreciate the other person's abundance of ideas, which he or she is willing to share with you. Be open to what that individual has to offer you, but remain in your positive feelings of abundance and confidence so that you can be discerning about the advice given.

One of my clients, Annette, was urged by a well-meaning friend, who was a real estate agent, to buy a house instead of continuing to rent. The agent insisted that Annette was losing a great deal of money by renting, and that she'd better act immediately or she'd lose even more. The friend didn't stand to gain financially from a sale, because she lived in a different city and wasn't going to make a commission. However, she had strong feelings of fear and unworthiness and was trying hard to convince Annette to buy a home in order to ease her own uncomfortable feelings. She also genuinely wanted to be of value to Annette and hoped to protect her from what she felt was a very real danger.

Annette listened to her friend's advice and thanked her for it, but she made a point of not becoming fearful or creating feelings of irritation or resentment as she was pressured. She valued her friend's love and kindness and expressed appreciation for it, knowing that as she did, she'd make it easier for her friend to replace feelings of unworthiness with feelings of worthiness. Then, Annette did more research, talked to her accountant and her banker, and ultimately chose to continue renting for a while and to focus on creating wealth, paying off her debts, improving her credit rating, and saving money for a down payment and closing costs. Annette's positive emotions allowed her to buy a house when she was ready to and not commit to a mortgage and high monthly payments. By remaining in a positive state, she was able to make the right choice for herself.

We all make more informed decisions, experience clarity, and manage our money much better when we operate from positive emotions. We create greater abundance for ourselves and others when we truly appreciate all the wealth we have in our lives and all that others have in theirs. Today, make a point of *appreciating.* Feel gratitude and increase the abundance in yourself and others.

I deeply appreciate all the love in my life. I am deeply valued and deeply blessed. I am rich with love and support. I am grateful for all the wisdom and resources available to me. I have a wealth of people who care about me and who enjoy seeing me experience abundance. I love to share my riches with them, and they love to return the favor.

I have unlimited possibilities before me. I enjoy boundless resources. I have wisdom and common sense. I am a gold mine of opportunity and wealth!

Distinction #14

Your Abundance Will Show Up for You in Exact Proportion to Your Belief about It

You are a money magnet. Are you a tiny refrigerator magnet that can barely keep a grocery list stuck to the surface, or are you such a powerful magnet that every paper clip in the house is flying through the air toward you and your force of attraction is even pulling the refrigerator across the floor in your direction?

The stronger your emotion of abundance, the stronger your money magnet. Don't think small. Make yourself the most powerful magnet you can be! Vibrate enormous abundance and be willing to accept all that the Universe can bring you. Don't say, "I only want a nice little starter home because that's a realistic goal." Let the Universe decide what's realistic. If you want a larger place, a great deal of financial holdings, and a fully funded college-savings account for your children, create the feelings you'd have if all that were yours right now and don't block the Universe from working with you to draw it in.

On the other hand, if you really prefer a smaller house because you'd be happiest in a cozy cottage with limited utility bills, low taxes, and fewer rooms to clean, then envision having that little home. The Universe will answer to all your desires, including that of living simply yet abundantly. Envision what *you* wish for most.

Maybe you envision owning a large home that's perfect for entertaining and filled with friends and family—and having enough money to pay the taxes and utilities and the salaries of people who can help you maintain it. Or you might desire extra bedrooms so that you can always host guests, or a beautiful old home that's been renovated to be highly energy efficient, with a roof garden and solar-powered electricity. Whatever you most value, affirm your right to it! Dream as big as you can and let the Universe surprise you with exactly how it fulfills your wish.

You might want to find photographs of what you most desire and what speaks to your heart and make a Dream Board to remind you of your vision. Gather pictures of what you'd like to attract, and print out words that resonate for you such as *security* and *home* and glue them to poster board. Put your Dream Board up on your wall, and as you look at it every day, create the emotions you would feel if you had all of those people, situations, and manifestations of abundance in your life right this moment.

If you'd like to have more money, and most of us do, go ahead and envision it coming to you, but don't limit yourself to a dollar amount. If you really need $5,000, you may well manifest that exact sum with the help of the Universe. But why not manifest $50,000? Or $500,000? One of my clients told me that when he says his affirmations, he states, "I easily write a check for my annual taxes, totaling a million dollars." I was intrigued by this and asked him why he would want to pay that much in taxes. He replied, "I can't even imagine how much money you'd have to have coming in to pay a tax bill of a million dollars!"

You might be surprised by how money comes in to you in the exact amount you need. One of my clients told me that she'd just sold her dining-room set for $400 one Sunday, and that evening there was a problem with her water heater, which was very old, and the emergency plumbing bill came to exactly

$400. At first, she felt upset that the money she'd just made left her wallet so quickly, but then she realized that the Universe had worked perfectly, finding her a buyer for her dining-room set just in time for her to pay the plumbing bill that would come due!

In fact, I've had this experience happen to me often: Years ago I spent a large sum of money on clothing to wear when I do public speaking, and as luck would have it, just as I was thinking, *Hmm, maybe I shouldn't have spent quite so much,* my accountant—who was preparing my taxes—called and advised me to pay myself that very amount to make up for my company having underpaid me. When unexpected expenses occur, we tend to focus on the negative and forget that unexpected gifts of abundance occur as well. That's part of the flow of wealth.

One of the ways I acknowledge and express gratitude for all that I have in my life and generate the powerful emotions of abundance, joy, and enthusiasm is through creating a Power Life Script. I've written, and will often update, an extensive list of affirmations that's so powerful that I consider it a script for the life I'm meant to live! I spare no details in describing the ideal circumstances of my life. I enthusiastically affirm all the forms of abundance I have and express gratitude for my family, friends, health, possessions, financial security, community, home, and more.

I've recorded my Power Life Script and listen to it when doing household chores, relaxing, or driving (currently, the recording runs about 27 minutes long). If you'd like to create your own Power Life Script, remember to be positive and specific and to write your affirmations in the present tense, saying, "I love to pay my bills easily and watch my net worth grow," not "I love knowing that I am going to get out of debt someday."

You can recite your Power Life Script each morning, or you can do what I do and record yourself reading it aloud with tremendous feeling, and then listen to it daily. As you say it out loud or listen to it, focus on creating the emotions you'd feel if all these circumstances were true right now. Feel the contentment, joy, enthusiasm, and gratitude you'd experience if you had that rapidly growing net worth and were easily paying all of your bills.

One obstacle to feeling gratitude and abundance that I often see people struggle with is lingering resentment over something that happened in the past that resulted in a diminishment of abundance. You must let go of the "loss"—whether it's a divorce, a drop in the value of a home or financial holdings, or a friendship that ended. When you remember that the Universe is continually giving and that you always have abundance that you can increase at any time, it's easier to let go of resentment. Learn what you can from the experience, and focus on what you *have,* not what you *had.*

A female client of mine years ago was married to a man who was very abusive to her because of his own insecurities. He wouldn't get therapy or examine his beliefs, feelings, and actions. After several years of listening to him cut her down, she decided to leave the marriage and quickly went from having a nonglamorous position in a company to being a very successful entrepreneur. Her ex-husband was so upset by his loss that he let his feelings of anger bleed over into every area of his life and poison his attitude. His friends began to avoid him, his children pulled away from him, and his boss found a reason to dismiss him. As a result, his finances took a nosedive. The angrier he got, the more financial and personal troubles he had. Sadly, he wasn't able to see that by clinging to the belief that he had suffered a tremendous "loss" and holding on to his resentment, he was creating more losses in his life. Vibrating feelings of lack and fear, he was co-creating situations that matched up with those feelings.

What he could have done instead was to see his "loss" as an opportunity for getting in touch with his abundance and his desires and cultivating his gratitude. After all, he had children who loved him, talents and skills, and health and wealth. If he valued and appreciated what he had, he could have created more happiness for himself and more abundance, including love. Unfortunately, his unwillingness to heal himself kept him in scarcity, fear, and anger, dwelling on his "loss."

Whatever you've lost you can regain in some form through the power of positive emotions. Trust that the Universe will give you all you desire, more than replacing any "loss" you've experienced, as long as you're willing to work with it and create more abundance within you.

I am grateful for all my opportunities for learning.
I have tremendous wealth within me, and I am nurturing it, growing it, and cultivating it, watching it expand more and more and more. My love expands. My trust expands. My confidence expands. My faith in the Universe expands.

My abundance is growing . . . growing . . . growing.
My riches are growing . . . growing . . . growing.

(**Note:** As you recite these affirmations, you may want to envision an ever-expanding balloon that can't pop or a plant growing ever larger as flower after flower opens into full bloom.)

A rainbow of abundance is mine. The colors are vivid and extraordinary. My rainbow of wealth expands outward, filling the sky with all its many shades and hues. My abundance comes in every color of the rainbow: red and pink and ruby, blue and sapphire and turquoise, green and evergreen and sea foam. I am filled with gratitude for the riches in my life. The Universe blesses me with this rainbow of abundance.

Distinction #15

THE LANGUAGE OF
ABUNDANCE IS POWERFUL

When people's flow of abundance is reduced to a trickle or wealth is moving away from them instead of into their life, notice what they'll say: "This always happens to me!" or "Just when I was getting ahead!" or "I can't hang on to money—I've always been a spender." It may be true that they haven't managed money well and have repelled it in the past, but when people validate a negative relationship to abundance, they create that reality in the present. Worse, they train themselves to believe that their situation at the moment is what it will *always* be, and that they'll *never* change it.

Be very careful of making sweeping negative generalizations about what "always" or "never" happens to you, and be aware of how you talk about money and the emotions that you create when you express what you're thinking about wealth and lack. Take financial responsibility for yourself, of course, and don't be in denial of your present situation . . . but when you talk about wealth, use language that signals to the Universe that you're on a new path. Words have tremendous power and energy, and the language you use to describe your financial situation actually creates feelings and vibrations that influence the Universe.

Take the word *broke*, as in "I'm broke!" It may be true that you have no money in your bank account and your salary isn't enough to cover the bills that are coming due this month. But are you "broken," like a doll lying helpless in a corner? Of course not! You always have resources, and you always have the ability to create positive emotions that will allow you to turn on the faucet of abundance.

Is money "tight," or are you tightly holding on to your ideas about how and when wealth should flow into your life and closing yourself off to the way the Universe wants it to flow? Instead of telling your partner, "Money's tight right now, so I'd like to postpone buying that item," say, "Yes, let's consider buying that item and talking about it while the money's coming in to us." In the real world, the cash for your new couch or car might not arrive for many months, but that doesn't mean you can't acknowledge that "the money's coming in to us"!

Are you really in a "financial crisis," meaning that you're on the brink of disaster . . . or are you on the brink of prosperity, poised to turn your financial situation around because you've finally woken up and become aware of how you've repelled money and how you can start attracting it? How you describe your situation, positively or negatively, will actually affect your ability to change it.

Many people are in the unconscious habit of talking negatively about money. Maybe you learned this from your parents and family. Mothers and fathers who have their own fears about money will often overreact when their child, who doesn't know about their financial situation, innocently asks, "Can I have that?" The usual response is: "No, we can't afford it!" The more fear a parent has, the more likely he or she is to deliver those words with fear and anger. Children get the message that they shouldn't wish or ask for what they want.

Rather than saying, "We can't afford it," a parent could guide kids in exploring why they would enjoy having that toy or piece of sports equipment and how they might create the abundance that would allow them to buy it. With our spouses, we'll often shut down our creativity rather than explore each other's dreams, desires, and possibilities. A negative word such as *can't* turns off the faucet of abundance and shut us down. Instead of saying, "We can't afford it," you can suggest, "Let's talk about ways we can afford it and whether this is what we really want."

If you're facing financial challenges, be honest about them and explore what your resources are. Generate positive emotions about wealth, but don't dwell on the difficulties and constantly discuss them. Talking to others about how in debt you are or how "times are tough" will increase your feelings of lack and fear. Remember that negative emotions and thoughts only serve one purpose—to help you learn. As soon as you've learned your lesson, get rid of those negative emotions and the words that express them. Make your decision about what you want to do, creating positive emotions, and you'll find yourself motivated to act in accordance with your new attitude and feelings about wealth. Your hope that your financial situation will get better will turn into faith.

A woman who heard me speak about wealth creation once asked me, "Should you tell others about your goals so that they hold you responsible for following through on them?" The answer is that it depends on how you think they'll respond and how you'll feel about that response. If you predict that they're likely to be encouraging, supportive, and positive, then go ahead and share your thoughts. But if you go around casually mentioning to people, "I'm going to invest in a new business," or "I've got a dream to travel to Paris," or you say this to someone who you know tends to be very fearful about money, you may very well get negative feedback. People may scoff or say, "How on earth are you going to afford that?" or "Oh, that's insanely expensive." If their response would make you feel doubtful, anxious, and foolish, don't tell them about your goal. Share your dreams only with those you can trust to support you. Affirm what you're going to do, but don't feel that you have to open yourself up to criticism and other people's negative feelings and beliefs.

Take a minute to go back to the list of terms meaning "wealth" that are in the Introduction to this book. Slowly read each out loud, and notice which ones are particularly powerful for you, helping you instantly create a feeling of abundance. Use these words whenever you create affirmations for yourself, and make them a part of your vocabulary when you talk about your own financial situation and goals for wealth creation. Use them to summon visual images of wealth that will inspire you to generate positive emotions. Draw on the power of the language of abundance to help you manifest all that you desire!

I love my lavish, luxurious, opulent life. I love my bulging wallet and the many figures in a row I see as I look at my checking and savings account balances. I love being a millionaire! I am a <u>billionaire!</u>

I am saturated with riches that I share with the world. I love being able to write a huge check to my favorite charity! I love being able to give to causes and projects I truly believe in. I relish knowing that I am lifting up others as I share my tremendous wealth! I see their smiles and rejoice at their excitement and abundance!

Distinction #16

ASK FOR WHAT YOU WANT
(ASK AND YOU SHALL RECEIVE)

The Bible says: "Ask, and it will be given to you; seek, and you will find; knock, and it will be opened to you." It sounds simple, doesn't it? But many of us hold hidden negative beliefs that prevent us from knocking on the door and asking the Universe for the wealth we desire.

HIDDEN NEGATIVE BELIEF #1:
"The Wealthy Aren't Good People"

When I was growing up, there were some children in our neighborhood who were often picked on, called names, and accused of being spoiled simply because their parents had money. It made me think that it must be awful to be rich. The children who teased these other kids didn't know any better because their parents had taught them to distrust wealthy people and be suspicious of them.

Not long ago, a friend of a friend was walking with me, and we passed a Lamborghini parked on the street. "I wonder what kind of crook that guy's got to be to own that car," he commented. Unfortunately, many people believe, as this man did, that if others have wealth, they must have come by it dishonestly.

Now, I've had the pleasure of working with many well-to-do people, and I have to say that often they're extremely generous, giving, and kind—yet this belief that the wealthy aren't good people persists. I think that it's because people are often secretly jealous of those who have wealth. Tearing others down and assuming the worst about them doesn't bring you any closer to riches or riches any closer to you. It will only cause you to feel negative emotions and to repel the wealth you desire.

Once, I was approached by a Christian organization that wanted to hire me for a project. I asked, "How can I serve you?"

The representative replied, "We'd like you to make one of our self-help books into a bestseller."

"I can definitely help you with that," I said enthusiastically. I've used my Internet-marketing skills and my passion to help many authors achieve that particular goal. I love lending my talents to projects that will allow others to learn, grow, and experience abundance.

"But," said the representative, "our author is a good Christian who insists that he doesn't want to become famous or make too much money."

I was curious: "Why wouldn't he want to be famous or to make money?"

My potential client explained to me that the author, like the members of the charitable organization he was a part of, felt that money and fame always leads to temptation and sin. He wanted his book to inspire people to change their lives for the better, but he didn't want to have to pay the price of becoming greedy, or "worldly."

"Well," I said, "I can't guarantee that he won't make money or be famous, and I feel strongly that if he's using his gifts and wisdom to serve, then the Universe is meant to respond by providing him with abundance in one form or another. Your author could always choose to give his money away to your organization."

The client saw my point, and in the end the author decided to donate all the profits for the book to the organization.

Along the way, many of us got the mistaken idea that we can't be trusted with a lot of money or influence—that wealth will make us into bad people somehow. We learned not to trust ourselves, so we put our light under a bushel and hid our gifts from the world. We need to let our light shine and accept the abundance that the Universe would like to give us.

HIDDEN NEGATIVE BELIEF #2:

**"I'd Have to Sacrifice Something of
Tremendous Value to Become Wealthy"**

My clients who resist the idea that they can be rich tell me that they fear the sacrifices they'd have to make in order to create wealth. A common fear is that they won't be able to spend time with their children because they'll have to work long hours to make a lot of money. I tell them that there are wealthy people who don't put in long hours and people who work extended hours engaging in wealth creation but who still find plenty of time to spend with their children. You don't necessarily have to give up your friends, family, health, or free time to experience great abundance. You're not limited in what you wish for! My Power Life Script, which affirms all the abundance I have and intend to have, includes affirmations of my health, my loving friends, time I invest in my relationships with my husband and with my son, and much more. You can wish for balance between personal time and work if you value that, and you can wish for many forms of abundance rather than just focusing on material wealth.

HIDDEN NEGATIVE BELIEF #3:
"To Acquire Wealth, I'd Have to Be Ruthless"

Like the man who felt that the owner of the Lamborghini had to have come by his money disreputably, you might be subscribing to the hidden—or not-so-hidden—belief that the only way to create wealth is by being cruel, selfish, and dishonest. This is a belief based in the false idea that there's a limited supply of abundance that we have to compete for. You don't have to outwit or outmaneuver the other guy to acquire the abundance you desire, because there's plenty of it for him and for you.

HIDDEN NEGATIVE BELIEF #4:

"If I Ask Others for Money, I'll Upset Them and They'll Become Angry with Me"

Even if you feel entitled to ask someone else for financial assistance, he or she may not feel that you're entitled to do so, and it's possible that the person might become angry with you because he or she feels that you're being disrespectful by asking. You're never responsible for others' feelings. What you *are* responsible for is truly valuing them and whatever help they can give you and changing your behaviors regarding money so that you don't end up in the same situation of neediness and lack again. After all, people want to help others make a permanent change for the better. They don't want to see their precious gifts squandered.

When you take on the responsibility for your actions and emotions, you'll find it easier not to feel guilty or ashamed for asking. One of my clients was in a relationship with a man from another country, and she was very uncomfortable when he lent a large sum of money to his cousin. She thought it was terrible that the cousin asked for the money given how hard her boyfriend had to work for it. She worried about whether the debt would be repaid and what would happen to her boyfriend if it wasn't, because he was working in his family's store and the money represented his entire financial cushion. Her boyfriend explained to her that in his culture, people lend large sums of money to their loved ones because it strengthens the bonds of family, and such loans are always repaid. He wasn't at all worried about his cousin paying him back, and in fact his cousin did repay him a couple of years later. The relative who borrowed the money hadn't been ashamed or guilty about asking for the loan because he had no doubt that he'd treat the money with respect, invest it wisely, and be able to return it.

On the other hand, sometimes when people lend money to a family member, their relationship with that person falls apart because the lenders feel that they aren't being respected for their generous act. The problem isn't that people sometimes can't meet their financial obligations to others; rather, it's that when they can't, they'll often allow their own feelings of embarrassment, shame, or fear prevent them from doing the right thing, talking to their family member or friend, and trying to repay the loan however they can. This is why people will say, "It's not the money I care about—it's the principle." We all want to feel that others are respecting us and, therefore, are appreciating and valuing the gifts we give them.

HIDDEN NEGATIVE BELIEF #5:
"I'm Not Worthy of Being Rich"

Some people resist wealth because they feel unworthy of it. They may have treated people badly in the past, and their guilt over their actions makes them feel awful about themselves and undeserving of abundance. They don't realize that they don't have to live in the past, and if they have unresolved feelings about what they did long ago, they can choose at any time to work through them and make amends to anyone they harmed. After doing so, it will be easier for them to forgive, love, and value themselves.

Others may have low self-esteem rooted in childhood that they may not even realize is there. Often people will cover up feelings of unworthiness by acting superior or cynical and tough. They fear looking at their painful underlying feelings of low self-worth, and this holds them back from experiencing positive emotions such as abundance. It can be difficult to access the hidden feeling of unworthiness, but it's important to do so in order to remove any blocks to attracting abundance.

HIDDEN NEGATIVE BELIEF #6:

"It Isn't Worth Putting Forth the Effort to Achieve Abundance"

Some people don't ask the Universe for wealth because they don't want to put forth any effort to grow their own abundance. They don't want to work or bring value unconditionally to the world, or engage in a creative process that might lead to a million-dollar idea, because they're willing to settle for what little they have. They don't realize that they're missing out on all the joy they could experience if only they would create positive feelings and allow enthusiasm to rise inside them and propel them forward. They also don't recognize that cultivating abundance is rewarding in itself regardless of how much money they end up generating.

Sometimes people with this hidden belief will start to become resentful and envious of those around them who do have wealth, convincing themselves that it's just bad luck that prevents them from enjoying abundance themselves. They'll adopt a victim mentality and not take responsibility for their emotions, attitudes, or behaviors. Unfortunately, they create their own reality of living in lack instead of creating the reality of living in abundance, which is their birthright.

Is it difficult for you to ask for abundance? Could it be because you're holding on to one of these false beliefs? Allow yourself to let go of it and replace your negative feelings with faith in the Universe. Then ask for what you desire.

One of my clients recently questioned me about whether it's appropriate to ask the Universe for what you'd like just once or if it's okay to do so again and again. I don't think it matters how often you put forth your request. What does matter are the emotions you create when you ask and the form of your asking. Don't acknowledge what you don't have and start generating a feeling of lack. For instance, don't petition the Universe to help you get out of debt or to bring you wealth in the future. The way to "ask" for what you want is by reciting a positive affirmation in the present tense. Affirm: "I am so excited to be increasing my wealth right now!"

If you feel funny affirming something because it doesn't feel true at the moment, remember that as you say these words with feeling, you'll be creating a vibration that alerts the Universe to bring you the abundance you desire. Draw on your imagination and create the powerful emotion of abundance. The more you generate this vibration, the clearer and louder your message to the Universe will be. Remember, too, to be patient and open as the Universe answers your affirmation in its own way, on its own timetable. Be open to its plan for you.

I am a wonderful, loving, generous, compassionate, and kind person. I am worthy of riches. I deserve to be wealthy and to live a life of opulence and luxury. I am entitled to be filled with abundance. I claim my birthright to prosperity and wealth right now. The Universe is increasing my riches at this very moment.

I appreciate my enormous wealth, and I am growing it right now. I am filled with joy, enthusiasm, and excitement as I work to bring value to the world. I enjoy the fruits of my labor.

Distinction #17

YOUR UNIQUE VALUES REGARDING WEALTH ARE IMPORTANT

As long as you're clear on what you most value and what you'd most like to create in your life, turning up the volume on your emotion of abundance will attract the wealth you desire, in the form of cash, people, situations, opportunities, or other resources. But if you let your fears get in your way, you'll start to place too much store in money and may begin violating your personal principles and brushing aside your unique values.

Fear can cause us to feel that we have to accumulate lots of money or financial security in order to be safe, but we can feel secure, cared for, loved, and trusting of the Universe without a lot of material wealth— and even without *any* material wealth. Create those positive feelings of safety and love and you won't give in to fear and start overvaluing money and thinking that it will soothe your anxieties and worries. When you're fearful, no amount of material prosperity will truly squelch that emotion. You can only address it with the antidote of faith.

Many people say that what's most precious to them is their relationships with their family and friends, yet when their fear flourishes, they begin to worry about money so much that they become short-tempered and obsessed with making more of it. Some men think that if their wives or children are unhappy, the solution is to be a better provider. Earning a larger income is one way to solve some problems in life, but it's not the only way to create a happy and loving family. Sometimes the best thing a man can do for his loved ones is to become a better provider of what his family needs most from him: his presence, affection, caring, and emotional support.

The majority of us would say that the most important thing in life is love, but when it comes to what else we value, we're all very different. Some people greatly prize adventure and the ability to travel. Others would like to have a life that's abundant with relationships. You may highly esteem learning, owning a large and beautiful home, having access to nature, or living a simple lifestyle. Whatever your values are, don't let worries about money distract you from what's most important to you. Replace your fear with faith that you'll be able to attain what you value. Faith, which is a positive emotion, will draw to you what you desire.

In the meantime, appreciate what you have now. If you're not living in the beautiful, large home you long for, be grateful for all the positive qualities of your current residence. If you live far away from nature, which you greatly value, enjoy the sparrows, grass, and small trees on your city block and make a point of spending time outdoors wherever you can. Trust that the more you acknowledge and feel gratitude for what you personally value, the more you'll increase it. Embrace and honor your unique values, whatever they are.

Never let someone else's values influence you to feel inferior about your own. Generally, if others are trying to make you feel bad about what you cherish, it's because they're feeling fearful about something. Their fear is *their* responsibility, and you don't have to respond to it by sharing this negative emotion. Instead, you might want to help them explore that fear by asking them about it, inquiring, "Why does it bother you that I'm spending my money on traveling [or collecting sports memorabilia/buying designer shoes/ giving to charities I believe in]? Do you wish you had more money to spend the way you'd like to?" Or you might ask them, "What is it about my business model that makes you so uncomfortable?" You might help them discover the hidden beliefs that are preventing them from manifesting wealth in their own lives or enjoying and sharing the abundance they have. Furthermore, their answers might help you clarify your own values and feel even more confident about your decisions.

I don't believe there's one correct way to spend or invest money. Everyone has different values, and as long as people are being true to them, and creating positive emotions instead of negative ones, I feel that they'll make the right decisions about money for themselves. Some experts on wealth creation say that you should take big risks, while others advise you to minimize them. Some say that it's a waste of money to buy a latte at a coffee shop every morning, but I say that if you truly savor that latte, and it helps you create an abundance of positive feelings, then that might be an excellent investment for you. Someone else might find that they create an abundance of positivity when they make their own coffee at home and carry it with them to the office, saving $3.75 a day and spending that money on something else that's important to them. I think that's terrific.

The book *The Millionaire Next Door* debunks a lot of myths about how millionaires supposedly live, and in my own experience, I've found that, indeed, some millionaires shop at Wal-Mart and buy their cars used. Never feel that you have to spend your money a particular way just because others say you do. I was amused to hear a friend of mine tell me that she bought her child used underwear and pajamas at a private school's rummage sale. She was thrilled to find nearly new, designer-brand boxer shorts for him for ten cents a piece, and she laughed when she overheard someone walking by muttering, "I would never buy used underwear!" She told me, "You know, that brand sells for $10.50 a pair, so I don't care what anyone else says, I feel great that I found such a bargain!" It takes confidence to stand by your own values regardless of what others say, but it's important to be true to them.

Then, too, if you truly treasure your spouse, your business partner, your roommates, or other important people in your life, honor their values as much as you do your own. One of my clients had a fairly high tolerance for risk, and she wanted an expensive, luxurious vehicle to drive. She really hoped to buy one car in particular and felt confident that her husband, who was up for a formal review at work in a few months and facing a possible promotion, would soon increase his income. If that happened, the car she wanted would be affordable for them.

However, her husband didn't have a high tolerance for risk. Much as he respected her desire for the expensive car, he didn't want to feel pressured to commit to a large monthly payment for it. Because their old car wasn't reliable or safe, the couple had to make a decision before knowing whether the promotion would come through. My client honored her husband's values by being conservative with their money and settling for a less fancy, used vehicle. She still firmly believes that he'll get his promotion and she'll get her nicer car, and she doesn't feel bad about her unique set of values just because they differ from her husband's.

If you're in conflict with someone who has different values, create positive feelings about your own as well as about his or her principles. In this way, you'll find it easier to be true to your values while honoring the other person's beliefs and finding common ground between the two of you.

Every human characteristic can be viewed in a positive or negative light. See the upside of others' qualities and you'll create positive feelings in yourself as well as making it easier for *them* to create positive feelings when they're around you. Value the differences between you and the people you care about and work with. Isn't it terrific that we all have our own gifts to offer each other?

The people in my life are gems. They are treasures and precious jewels. I am so grateful for their love, kindness, and support. I cherish the wonderful qualities of the people in my life. I notice and appreciate their unique attributes, just as I do mine.

I love being able to manage and spend my money the way I want to. I am thrilled that I am in harmony with the important people in my life. Together, we make terrific decisions about how we are going to use our mutual riches.

Distinction #18

THERE IS AN ABUNDANCE OF
RESOURCES AVAILABLE TO EVERYONE

Each of us has valuable resources to appreciate and share with others, but too often we overlook our own and others' riches, especially if they take an unexpected form. When we face a challenge, we're likely to look to our usual sources of abundance, and if they aren't available to us, we don't know where to search next. We don't see the resources right in front of our eyes.

I remember watching the movie *The Pursuit of Happyness,* which is based on a real story about a man named Chris Gardner who struggled to take care of his young son while homeless and trying to better his situation. It's an inspiring story of dreaming big and persevering, but as I watched the main character in the film, played by Will Smith, desperately looking for a place where he and his son might be able to sleep for the night, I wondered, *Is he really using all his resources? Doesn't he have any friends or family to call? Isn't there a social services agency that could help him find a place where he and his son could both stay? Why not knock on the door of strangers and see if they could take his son and him in or help in some way?* Being self-directed can be a wonderful quality, but we don't always have to solve all our own problems.

Even if we were to run out of money or credit, most of us have someone who can help us out in some way, if only we would just ask for assistance. Look at how complete strangers responded to the Hurricane Katrina disaster with money and practical aid, even offering their spare bedrooms to those who were left homeless. People were incredibly resourceful in finding ways that they personally could help the residents of New Orleans and other areas that were devastated by the storm.

If you doubt your resources and feel that your abundance is limited, think about the people in your life and what they have to offer you and what they have offered you in the past. Maybe you said no to them because you wanted to do things all on your own, but in a pinch you could come to them for assistance. Think about all the resources in your neighborhood—

whether it's a small-business association or a chamber of commerce that can help you in starting an enterprise, a library with staff who can help you find information, or a community center where you can take low-cost classes and develop skills for creating and managing wealth.

Often when people are in need, they create negative feelings about themselves and their situation and decide that if they refuse help, they'll feel stronger and more powerful. There's no shame or weakness in accepting assistance. All situations are temporary, and there's no reason why the flow of abundance in your life can't be increased. All you have to do is turn on the tap and be open to receiving what it yields. Feeling bad about yourself will simply block your receptivity.

A friend of mine had very little training in accounting or money management but was able to become quite financially successful. Still, he felt that he didn't have the skills to invest his money well, so he hired a financial advisor to help him. However, he didn't create feelings of inadequacy simply because he didn't have investment expertise and knowledge. He simply dealt with his situation in a practical way, hiring help, and then began the process of developing his skills. He read dozens of books on financial management and investing and then imagined what his investments might be. For a year, he watched his imaginary investments flourish, and at the end of the year, he compared them with the ones his financial manager had made for him. His investments would have done better, so he took over his own accounts and said good-bye to his advisor. I'm so proud of him for taking the initiative to learn about financial management himself rather than creating negative thoughts such as *I can't do this; I have to leave it to professionals.*

There is no one right investment strategy for everyone. One size does not fit all! To make the right decisions for *you,* be aware of your unique values regarding money, and be conscious of your resources rather than taking them for granted. Often people who win the lottery will spend everything and end up right where they started financially because they begin to think they have all the resources in the world, when actually the amount of money they have is limited (even if there's quite a lot of it). They don't respect their resources by learning how to manage the money and will therefore spend it all quickly, often buying a big, expensive house and not accounting for upkeep costs— from utilities and maintenance to property taxes.

Respecting your resources means honoring your abundance rather than squandering it without thinking. Be conscious of how much you have at the moment and appreciate it: Be grateful for it, and cultivate it so that it can grow even more.

A terrific way to learn how to be more conscious of your resources is to start keeping track of all the money you spend. This task can be time-consuming, but there are computer programs that can help, and if you use debit and credit cards, you'll have a clearer record of where your money goes. It takes a commitment of time and effort to watch where every penny goes for a month, and it also can be a challenge to resist judging yourself or feeling scared as you start to see just how much you're spending. Notice the negative feelings you create about money, and learn from them if you can (maybe the lesson is that you really don't want to maintain the habit of devoting your last minutes before bedtime to browsing Internet shopping sites!). Self-correct your spending if it feels right to do so, but don't get caught up in judging yourself.

The main purpose of this exercise is simply to become aware of what you're spending money on. Once you've tallied it all up, sit down—with your partner, if you have one—and analyze where your finances are going. Consider whether your habits are in sync with your unique values regarding wealth or whether they're just unconscious patterns. Ask yourself, *What can I do to change those habits to make them more in line with how I actually want to spend my money?*

Honoring resources also means respecting that the flow of abundance isn't necessarily predictable and isn't always completely in your control. It's not forever streaming toward you and into you at full force. Sometimes the flow is a trickle or is even moving away from you. It could be because you're experiencing negative feelings that are blocking you, but it may be that you're not the only creative force in the Universe. Stuff happens, as they say.

The other day I discovered that my lawn was infested with bugs, and when I asked the neighbor's gardener what he thought we ought to do to get rid of them, he said that we should tear up our entire lawn and reseed. That solution would cost thousands of dollars. My husband, Denis, became upset because we spend money on regular lawn care and even so are having problems that might cost us a lot. I reminded him that there's no value in harboring negative feelings about this challenge. By creating a sense of faith, abundance, and curiosity, we came up with the idea to call our lawn-care service and ask for advice. They told us that our service contract guarantees that they'll solve any insect-infestation problems, so we don't have to spend any money after all. This was a possibility that we didn't think of at first. We were blind to a resource we already had—a legal guarantee provided by our service.

Then, too, all of us interact with each other and influence one another's flow of abundance to some degree, and yours may lessen or reverse directions because of forces outside of your control that are created by another person or other people. When the stock market shifts downward and the interest rates go up because of situations you have no influence over, acknowledge and make use of the power you do have: that of your positive emotions. Create even stronger feelings of faith and abundance. Open your eyes to the resources and opportunities you've been overlooking and make the most of them. Remember that even during the Great Depression and in times of recession, there has been a flow of abundance, and some people were quite prosperous. Nurture the abundance you have right now and let go of your attachment to the abundance that has flowed away from you.

Honoring and respecting your resources may mean recognizing at last that the skills you've voluntarily lent to nonpaying projects are worthy of compensation. Maybe you can convert your hobby into a paid job. Then, too, use your time and energy wisely, as these are also valuable assets. Network with other people, exchange resources and information, and discover ways to appreciate and grow each other's abundance.

Respecting resources also means being frugal instead of wasteful. If something doesn't have value for you, don't spend money on it, even if you *have* the money for it. It's easy to fall into spending habits and not stop to say, "Gee, I don't need this service anymore—I'm really not using it," or "I think I could get a better price than I'm getting if I check around." If you're not watching television these days, are you paying for movie channels and on-demand services that you don't need? If your cell-phone bill keeps creeping up, do you really have to make that many calls on your cell, and if so, could you negotiate a better pricing package? If you're living in a house or apartment that's larger than you need it to be, are you truly appreciating it, or would you have more appreciation for a smaller home that's more suited to your lifestyle right now? Ask yourself, *Do I really value this, or am I just unconsciously spending money?*

Just as you wouldn't leave a faucet dripping, costing you money and wasting resources, don't squander the resources you have. Use them for something you value. By constantly creating feelings of abundance and faith that the Universe will provide, you can ensure that your resources will always be there for you and that you're working with the Universe to co-create even more abundance for yourself and others.

I open my eyes, my heart, and my arms to all the re-sources and assistance available to me. I am patient and trusting as I watch the stream of abundance flow into me, its force growing stronger and stronger. I feel the rush of it pouring into my life from all directions.

Every pore in my body opens to the abundance that flows in. I am grateful for all this bounty—for this river of liquid gold and silver pouring into me. I claim my wealth. I claim my riches. Thank you, Universe, for such tremendous abundance coming to me from every direction!

Distinction #19

WEALTH COMES IN MANY FORMS

My mentor, Bob Proctor, once said, "Don't cry over anything that won't cry over you." People will often create tremendous suffering for themselves just because they're in debt or have lost money. They'll generate intense feelings of anger, sadness, and fear, all of which are destructive and actually make it more difficult for them to regain the wealth they lost. Because they're upset, they may fight with their spouse over money or become severely depressed, not realizing that the power to create abundance for themselves once again is always available to them.

When you understand that money is simply one form of the tremendous force known as abundance or wealth, and that you can always receive riches from our ever-giving Universe, it becomes easier to let go of negative feelings about money and the destructive belief that material wealth is more important than other manifestations of abundance. Ask yourself how much money you would take in exchange for your eyesight and your abundant health. How much would I have to pay you for you to give up your relationship with the person you love the most? My guess is that your health, your eyesight, and the people you love are far too precious to trade for any amount of money.

If what you receive isn't money, open yourself up to it with gratitude and joy. Allow your creativity to flourish and you can discover ways to convert the abundance into the form you could most use right now.

Wisdom and knowledge are types of abundance that we often overlook. An antiques dealer I know often purchased items from homeless people who brought him furniture and other objects they'd found in the garbage. He was always gracious and kind to them, and one day one of his regular sellers, who was a homeless man, noticed that the dealer had recently acquired a gold record by a celebrity. "You have that underpriced," he said. "I used to work in the music business. I know." The antiques dealer listened to what the man had to say and decided to take his advice and quadruple the price. A few days later, the dealer's dentist came in, got very excited about the gold record, and said, "Listen, I'd love to own that, but I don't have that much in cash to spend. How about if I do that dental work I recommended to you, in exchange for the gold record?" The antiques dealer was able to pay for expensive dental procedures he needed and couldn't afford, because he valued the abundance that came to him from an unexpected source and converted it into something he could use.

Knowledge and wisdom is all around us, but too often we don't take the time to explore, research, listen, and consider because we focus too much on wealth in the form of money. Older people often have very valuable insights that can save us financially. Friends can have knowledge we're unaware of that they'd love to share if only we'd be open to hearing what they have to say.

I once had a neighbor who loved to talk about remodeling, and I gave him the gift of letting him share his enthusiasm with me. One day he told me that the local inspection ordinances caused home owners to spend far more money on remodeling than they would have to if they lived in the next county. It was a valuable piece of information that I factored in when I bought property and that I passed along to another friend who was considering remodeling and possibly moving. By being open to the possibility that what someone has to share may benefit us in some way, we remain open to the ingenious forms of abundance that the Universe is trying to bestow upon us.

When we have faith that the Universe is working to bring us the wealth we desire, it's easier to create feelings of creativity and kindness that open us up to opportunities for increasing our abundance. Miracles may even happen, if we're open to them.

If you find yourself uncomfortable with the generosity of others, accept their gift with joy and gratitude and let go of any feelings that you're un-worthy of it. In receiving, you're actually giving them a gift as well: You're allowing them to experience the joy of giving and the feeling of being so abundant that they can share their wealth with you. Remember, too, that the flow of abundance is continuous. Know that you can pass along a great deal to someone else, and they'll pass it along to yet another person. Let the river of abundance flow through you, trusting that as it moves in and out of your life, it will benefit you and the world. Enjoy its twists and turns and appreciate the magical way in which it works.

*The river of abundance is flowing into my life, surging
with energy, and I feel it filling me up with wealth.
It is wonderful to be so rich! I feel expansive! I
choose to share all these riches! I open myself
up to receive even more wealth.*

*I am thrilled to be co-creating abundance in the Universe
in so many ways. I love watching how the Universe works
with me in our creation. I am inspired by its creativity!
I open myself to all the abundance it is pouring
into me. Thank you, Universe, for blessing
me with this tremendous wealth!*

Distinction #20

Right Now, You Have the Wisdom Within You to Be Rich

Often people assume that to achieve success and wealth, you need a high level of intelligence, but it's not true. There are many unemployed Ph.D.'s—and yet both Bill Gates and Steve Jobs, who revolutionized the computer world and brought PCs into people's homes, had dropped out of college. Each of us has within us the wisdom to be rich. It is our inborn ability to use our accumulated knowledge and common sense to make sensible, good judgments that allow us to attract the abundance we deserve.

You may think that you don't have this wisdom, but you do. We all do. When we were young, we learned the basics of acquiring and maintaining wealth: Don't regularly have more flowing out than you have flowing in. Save for a rainy day. Invest wisely.

Don't overspend. So why do people who may even be very smart and successful in other areas of their lives get into so much trouble with money, acquiring debt and spending so much that they create an imbalance in the flow of wealth in and out of their lives?

It's because they're blocked from their natural wisdom by feelings of fear, scarcity, jealousy, anger, unworthiness, and sadness. They don't have the power of love, joy, enthusiasm, or faith strongly influencing their spending, saving, or investing habits. If they did, they would be creative and discerning about where their money and resources flowed.

We manage the flow of abundance wisely when we're in a state of positivity, like a gardener who carefully positions the sprinkler or aims a garden hose in the direction of the flowers instead of toward the sidewalk. We find creative ways in which to increase our wealth when we're feeling enthusiastic, calm, or happy. But when we're experiencing negative emotions, we build a brick wall between ourselves and our wisdom. Caught up in our strong emotions, we can't think straight, draw upon our knowledge, and make good judgments. We forget that we have the power to turn on the faucet of abundance and to influence its flow.

Many of us weren't taught by our parents or schoolteachers how to manage money. Maybe you learned how to balance a checkbook from the account manager at the bank the very first time you opened a checking account and never quite got the hang of it until a friend showed you what you were doing wrong. Maybe when you got your first job, a wise older sibling told you to take some money, even just a small amount, out of each paycheck and put it in a pretax account matched by your employer. Perhaps no one ever taught you how credit cards or interest work, or you can't figure out why you keep overdrawing your checking account. Or, maybe you were never "book smart" and are intimidated by such terms as *prime rate, variable interest, bonds,* and the like. If you give in to your discomfort and fears about managing money, you'll block yourself from learning how to manage it.

Today, you may not have the knowledge you need to handle your money well, or you may need to learn to manage it even better; most people do. We live in the information age, and there's plenty of advice and guidance available to us. Bookstores stock many volumes on money management. People make careers out of lecturing, coaching, and advising others on how to use their resources wisely, investing in ways that build financial security. Daily newspapers often have entire sections about money and finance that are chock-full of clever tips and advice.

I personally find a lot of money-management advice unexciting and even confusing, but I've made a point of hiring a financial planner who can explain finances to me in a way I can understand, and he's so enthusiastic about the prospect of helping me grow my wealth that he gets me to feel excited about it, too. Find a person, a book or books, a magazine, or a Website that gets you feeling positive about mastering the art of managing wealth—they're out there!

I believe that sometimes even the most conscientious and responsible people who have studied money management make mistakes, spending lavishly and then experiencing buyer's remorse or investing too quickly without checking the fine print or asking enough questions. These types of mistakes happen because people aren't allowing themselves to notice their negative emotions, explore them, and learn what lessons these feelings hold for them.

If you're uneasy about an investment, purchase, or loan, pay attention to that feeling. Sit with it, and don't let yourself feel rushed. Create a sense of calm. Then ask yourself, *What is it about this purchase, investment, or loan that doesn't feel right?* Don't be afraid of the answer, which may be one of the following:

- I feel pressured to invest in order to please my financial advisor, who is very enthusiastic about this opportunity. I'm feeling fearful, not confident.

- I feel resentful buying this item I don't really want, but I'm afraid my spouse will be angry with me if I question this purchase or say no.

- I feel scared because I don't really understand this investment, and I don't have faith in my ability to learn more about it so that I can make an informed decision.

You have much wisdom, and that nervous feeling in your gut, the tension in your neck, and the second thoughts that keep popping up at odd moments are all messages from your wise self, saying, *Look again, but more closely this time.*

When you let go of your fear of experiencing difficult emotions, you break down the brick wall between you and your natural wisdom about acquiring and maintaining wealth. Then you can let go of unproductive thoughts such as: *I'm no good at this "money" stuff,* and *I don't trust myself investing,* and *I can't be trusted with too much cash—I'll just spend it all.* You can reclaim your power to create positive emotions about abundance and open the faucet of plenty so that riches flow into your life.

One effective technique for uncovering any hidden thoughts or beliefs that are causing you to cut off the flow of abundance is to keep a daily Assets and Liabilities Journal. Open the journal and on the left side of the page, note all the positive emotions and thoughts you're experiencing regarding money, prosperity, wealth, and abundance. Also jot down any actions you take that are in alignment with your desire to live according to the 21 Distinctions: to provide value and to embrace that which the Universe sends your way. Feelings, beliefs, and actions that are in harmony with abundance have tremendous value and draw in even more wealth and riches, so count them as "assets."

On the right side of the page, note your liabilities—that is, any negative emotions or thoughts you experienced that day regarding money and prosperity, as well as any actions you took that were out of sync with your desire to live according to the 21 Distinctions. Mention which feelings were connected to those thoughts and actions, because emotions are very powerful and can actually change your vibration so that you either attract abundance or repel it.

Looking at what you've written on the right side of the journal page, consciously choose to let go of any feelings of self-judgment you might be experiencing, as they'll only lead to more negative feelings—not to positivity, creativity, and openness to learning. On the other hand, honestly assessing your thoughts, feelings, and behaviors that contribute to feelings of lack and a vibration of scarcity will help you change how you think, feel, and behave. After all, if you don't realize you've fallen into a bad habit, how can you change it?

Try starting an Assets and Liabilities Journal and see what you can learn from it. Letting go of any tendency to judge yourself, honestly record what you did, felt, and thought today about abundance, simply noticing these things. Then ask yourself whether your liabilities are stronger and more numerous than your assets—or do you simply need to be more aware each day of your negative feelings, beliefs, and actions so that you can quickly replace them with more positive ones?

Your own page might read something like this:

Assets	Liabilities
I wrote out my financial goals 20 times. With great conviction, I read all of my affirmations about prosperity and created positive feelings about my ability to draw in the wealth I know I deserve. I paid my bills, and I did so with gratitude for all the wealth I have. I did a visualization exercise, imagining a waterfall of riches pouring into me and flowing outward from me, and I pictured myself writing a check to pay off my credit card debt, savoring the wonderful feeling of prosperity that I created in me. I carefully evaluated an investment, and I looked for more investments. I considered two options at the grocery store and chose the one that was of better quality even though it cost more, because I know I'm worth it and so is my family.	*I spent too much money today on frivolous things, and I felt bad about it. I was in a spending mode, and by the end of the day, I was feeling out of control. I felt guilty for wasting money and scolded myself for buying so much. I made a deposit on a vacation without price shopping and comparing. I felt anxious about the thought of where the money would come from to pay for the trip, and I worried that I wouldn't be able to take a vacation at all if I didn't move quickly and book it. I impulsively overtipped the waitress at lunch because I felt I had to impress my lunch date, and I was upset with myself for doing so. I was out of control with my spending and feeling a lot of guilt, lack, and fear.*

Again, I won't tell you a right or wrong way to manage your money. In this example, someone else might not have felt guilty overtipping the waitress. The idea is to observe which emotion you were feeling and operating from when you spent the money. If overtipping the waitress made you feel terrific because you were able to share your wealth with someone who also made you feel special and valued, your expenditure at lunch would belong on the left side of your page with your assets. By recognizing when and why you're creating negative feelings and thoughts about abundance, you can begin to change them and act in accordance with the 21 Distinctions of Wealth.

I am experiencing great abundance, and I revel in my riches. I take ownership of my wealth. I am the wise steward of my finances, the gardener who cares for all my riches. I enjoy learning about wealth, cultivating it, growing it, and sharing it. I value all that I have, and I nurture and tend my garden. I love to exchange ideas about increasing prosperity. I love to learn more about how to maintain my very healthy financial situation and expand my riches further. I have tremendous respect for all my resources.

I have a treasure chest full of resources available to me at all times. I immerse my hands in its riches, eager to touch, feel, and experience my wealth as I imagine how to exchange it, grow it, and give it back to the ever-providing Universe. I am deeply grateful for all the incredible affluence I have.

Distinction #21

WEALTH CONSCIOUSNESS LEADS TO WEALTH-GENERATING ACTIONS

Deepak Chopra said that if you want to be rich, you must first be rich in consciousness. Consciousness is an awareness of what you have and what you *can* have if you're willing to dream big, and it helps you to co-create whatever you desire. It's the soil in which you can plant your seeds of prosperity.

Wealth consciousness is also the awareness of the nature of abundance, and of your ability to work with its flow to manifest riches in your life. Once you have this mind-set, no one can take it away from you, and you can use it at any time. The only thing blocking you from attaining it is old habits of thinking, feeling, and behaving—habits that you can consciously choose to replace so that it feels easy and natural to maintain an attitude of wealth consciousness. In this state, you'll be able to easily access the enthusiasm and drive to act in ways that foster and nurture your abundance.

However, even if you're in a state of wealth consciousness most of the time, you'll still have to act. Action is key to manifesting your dreams in the physical world. I spent many years reading self-help books, attending lectures on empowerment by all sorts of inspirational speakers, and listening to every self-improvement tape I could find . . . but none of this mattered until I finally had an epiphany: *Understanding isn't enough. You have to apply what you know.*

The key to a treasure chest does you no good if you don't put it in the lock and turn it. You can memorize all 21 Distinctions of Wealth, but you won't experience their power until you apply them to your life and live by them.

The way to lasting change is through creating habits, and that's why it's so important to commit yourself to creating the habit of growing your abundance and following a program for developing the 21 Distinctions of Wealth. I explained this program in the Introduction of this book, and you can use the checklists at the back and available on my Website (**www.destinies.com**) to help you stay on track. No amount of intellectual understanding of the

Distinctions can substitute for developing the habit of living by them.

As you go about your day, reciting your affirmations at least three times (in the morning, once during the day, and at night), remember that it's important to remain aware of the flow of wealth. Create and use the Assets and Liabilities Journal described in Distinction #20 to help you do so. Then, as you become more conscious of any negative attitudes about wealth and abundance you're experiencing, you'll probably notice that you're more likely to engage in them, and the negative feelings they create, in certain situations.

Consider limiting your exposure to these situations. If talking about money with your financial advisor, spouse, friend, or parent always makes you feel guilty and ashamed, consider whether his or her approach is making it difficult for you to let go of those emotions and experience positive ones as you make financial decisions. You might want to explore the ways in which you can discuss money together without your feeling drawn into negativity, and you might choose to stop discussing money with him or her altogether if that's appropriate (for instance, you may want to hire a new financial advisor or not talk about your financial decision making with your friend or parent).

Be aware of your resources—the gold beneath the Buddha's surface—and the flow of wealth in your life. Be conscious of how you're spending and investing your abundance. Most important, know your emotions so that you can be sure you're creating the powerful positive ones that will increase your abundance. All of us can fall into old habits or become unconscious during the course of our busy days. Cultivate awareness, but if you should happen to notice that you're back to the old pattern of worrying about your debt or spending money out of a sense of lack, don't judge yourself and feel that you've failed somehow. Simply shift back into wealth consciousness and immediately change your behavior, recommitting to living by the 21 Distinctions of Wealth.

As you create greater success for yourself, you may find that you start taking it for granted and stop being aware and appreciative of the abundance in your life. Often businesses that grow quickly will begin taking their client base for granted, providing less customer service than they did when they first started out. This lax attitude toward the rich resource of customers will result in a business's abundance slipping away, as customers move on to another company that's more respectful of them.

In your personal life, too, you might start to

assume that the tremendous flow of abundance you're experiencing right now will always continue at the current rate, and forget how important it is to respect and nurture all your resources. If you have financial holdings available for the periods when your abundance flow slows down due to circumstances beyond your control, you'll find it much easier to increase that flow again quickly because you'll take comfort in knowing that you have enough resources to carry you through the challenging times.

Whenever you want to grow your abundance, reconnect to the flow and appreciate and nurture others' abundance as well. Years ago my friend had a job in a small retail shop that couldn't possibly compete with a rival store's prices because her store didn't have as much buying power, but my friend's manager was determined to increase profits. He called together his team of workers, many of whom were teenagers, and told them he wanted them to help him sell more products so that all of them could experience greater prosperity. He promised to increase their hours and wages if the team was successful, and he told them he felt great confidence in their abundance of abilities. He built up their positive feelings and presented his plan for providing better customer service than their rival store offered.

One aspect of the plan was that if anyone running a register noticed more than two people in line at another register, they were to make an announcement calling customers to come to theirs to check out. Soon customers realized that while the prices were higher there than at the other store, they could consistently get in and out quickly, and they began going where my friend worked instead of the cheaper store. In a few short months, the clever manager announced to his team that their store had experienced a tremendous leap in profits. He followed through on his promises, and the success continued to grow. He couldn't have achieved his goal without having a wealth consciousness that he invited his team to share with him, nor could he have done it without everyone being conscious and committed and following through with their plan.

So value and honor your resources, including the wisdom that you've just acquired in this book. Create positive feelings about the 21 Distinctions, establish the habit of wealth consciousness, and share your enthusiasm and abundance with others. Stop to feel gratitude as you see the seeds of wealth sprouting up in your life and as riches begin to manifest all around you, creating a lush garden for you to savor and appreciate. Act in accordance with wealth consciousness and enjoy the feeling of being wealthy!

*Right now I am aware of all the prosperity in my life.
I am conscious of my potential to grow riches, and I am
watering my wondrous, lush garden of abundance.*

*I am committed to creating wealth. I am committed to
honoring and respecting all the wonderful resources I
have—to growing the seeds of my possibilities. Every day,
I manifest wealth with my thoughts, feelings, and actions.*

AFFIRMATIONS FOR THE

21 Distinctions of WEALTH

AFFIRMATIONS FOR DISTINCTION #1:

You Are Already Rich—
You Were Born That Way!

- *A shimmering, golden fortune is mine.*

- *Wealth flows into me like a fertile river, nurturing me, enriching me, and helping me produce all that I desire.*

- *Inside me is sheer opulence. I am filled with riches, teeming with possibilities. My tremendous wealth is flowing forth, nourishing my life and nourishing everyone around me.*

- *I have always had all the wealth that I need. I savor the riches that are my birthright.*

AFFIRMATIONS FOR DISTINCTION #2:

The Willingness to Give It All
Up Leads to Having It All

- *My wealth takes many forms. I tend a beautiful, lush garden that bursts into bloom in the sunshine. I have faith that I am growing richer every day in many ways.*

- *Abundance and prosperity are always available to me. I have complete confidence in my ability to foster and create wealth. I am always wealthy.*

- *Riches flow into my life. I allow them to come to me from all directions, to wash over me, and to fill me up. I am saturated with wealth.*

- *I allow abundance to pour into my life, and I open myself to the Universe's bounty. Wealth comes to me at the exact time I need it. I have as much money as I need, and more.*

AFFIRMATIONS FOR DISTINCTION #3:

There Is an Infinite
Supply of Abundance

- *The fertile waters of wealth flow into me, through me, out of me, and back into me, connecting me with all the abundance in the Universe. I savor these waters. I drink deeply from the spring of abundance, and I feel nourished. I am saturated and overflowing with riches.*

- *I breathe in and fill myself with all the abundance the Universe has available to me. Naturally, easily, I draw in the wealth I deserve. I express my prosperity, giving freely, with love and enthusiasm. I have plenty. I am blessed with riches. Money pours into my life, and I share my riches with the world. I love being wealthy.*

AFFIRMATIONS FOR DISTINCTION #4:

The Universe Is Always Giving

- *What an incredible bounty I am enjoying! The Universe is overflowing with gifts for me. I hear the knocking at the door, and I open it to receive a shower of prosperity. I open my arms and receive all the gifts of the Universe with gratitude, enthusiasm, and joy. I feel lucky!*

- *I am delighted to see all that the Universe has for me! My wealth comes in many forms. The Universe knows just what I need and brings abundance in an infinite number of ways.*

- *I am worthy of prosperity and abundance. I deserve the best of the best, and I am deeply grateful for all my wealth. I love experiencing the abundance that belongs to me. I am the owner of the finest, most wonderful home. I dine on the most delicious meals every day. I savor every bite. I am deeply thankful for the opportunities and choices that I have and for my freedom. I am deeply thankful for the abundance of love in my life. I deserve to be rich! I am rich!*

AFFIRMATIONS FOR DISTINCTION #5:

When You Let Go of Envy, You Let Go of Ignorance

- *I have all that I could ever want. The Universe answers my joy with more joy, my abundance with more abundance. I am thrilled to see what the Universe is bringing me right now! I am open to all the fantastic, ingenious possibilities it has created for me.*

- *As I look around me at all the wealth others enjoy, I feel tremendous excitement for them and for myself, because I know that I, too, have overflowing abundance. I live a life of luxury and opulence. I appreciate all the gifts the Universe gives to me and to everyone around me. It is fantastic to live in a world of wealth and riches! I claim mine today. I deserve abundance. It is washing over me right now, filling me up with a sense of richness and gratitude.*

- *I love my home . . . and all the wonderful gifts I have. . . . I am deeply grateful for all my wealth.*

AFFIRMATIONS FOR DISTINCTION #6:

All the Riches You Haven't Recognized or Claimed in the Past Are Still Available to You

- *Every day new ideas and opportunities come to me. My inner wealth attracts increasing prosperity each day. My abundance is growing inside me and pulling in more and more riches, like a powerful magnet. I feel alive and excited by all the wealth that is in my life and all that is on its way to me!*

- *I am deeply grateful for all the opportunities I have been given in my life. I have learned wonderful lessons that serve me well as I continue to expand upon all the riches I have. I have always been wealthy. I will always be wealthy! Wealth is mine!*

- *Today I open my eyes to the abundance before me. I discover the value I have been overlooking, and I rejoice at finding it again. I am so exited to reclaim my wealth!*

AFFIRMATIONS FOR DISTINCTION #7:

Infinite Patience Produces
Immediate Results

- *The Universe operates with perfect timing, and I completely trust in it. The wisdom of the Universe is infinite. I am working with the Universe and creating wealth right now. I am enjoying the many ways in which the Universe is manifesting riches for me!*

- *Money is the rushing stream of water from the melting snow at the top of the mountain. It scrambles over rocks and soil and hurries to meet me. Wealth invigorates me as it flows into my life! I am excited to be rich!*

- *As I practice supreme patience, I enjoy the riches that the Universe is manifesting in my life at this very moment. Thank you, Universe, for the tremendous abundance I have right now. I possess so much of value already! I have so many loving friends and family members in my life. I have an affectionate, caring partner who truly values me and reminds me of all my many gifts. I have an abundance of love and joy. I feel tremendous gratitude. I have amazing talents and skills. I am greatly appreciated for the work I do. I have endless creativity, and I am always open to the many possibilities that are available to me at all times.*

- *I am grateful for my excellent credit rating and my extremely high income that gives me tremendous wealth that flows forth from me and enriches others. I am grateful for my beautiful, opulent home and the bounty of healthful food I enjoy. I am so lucky to be in fantastic health. All my blessings attract more blessings. All my love attracts more love. All that I deserve—all that I desire—is flowing into my life at this very moment, and I receive it with deep gratitude and open arms.*

AFFIRMATIONS FOR DISTINCTION #8:

You Don't Have to Know How You'll Get What You Want— You Just Have to Decide *What* You Want

- *Abundance is everywhere, and it is showing up in my life right now. The Universe provides money and riches to me in countless clever ways. I love to see all the many avenues the Universe creates in order to bring me even more wealth. I open my eyes to the opportunities the Universe creates for me and the possibilities it presents to me. Thank you, Universe, for all these wonderful opportunities and all this wonderful wealth flowing into my life.*

- *All around and inside of me are resources I can use and exchange at any time. Within me is a gold mine. Everywhere I look, I see my resources, wealth, and prosperity. I have so much to give! I have so much to exchange! I love being rich!*

AFFIRMATIONS FOR DISTINCTION #9:

The More Value You Give Unconditionally, the More You'll Have

- *My work, ideas, skills, and talents are of great value. I have an infinite amount of abundance and worth. I have many blessings, and I love to share them with others. I have an extraordinary supply of love, and I give love unconditionally. I am a valuable contributor to the world, which appreciates all that I do and gives back to me continually. The Universe is bestowing great abundance on me, showering me with love and blessings.*

- *I have so much to offer to the world, and I am giving it freely, from my heart. I give with passion, joy, and enthusiasm. I love sharing what I have. I am thrilled that I am inspiring others, and I rejoice at how they inspire me. I get excited thinking about all the many ways that value is flowing back into my life every minute of every day. I love receiving all the unexpected gifts that the Universe gives to me. I am so blessed!*

AFFIRMATIONS FOR DISTINCTION #10:

All of Your Positive Emotions Positively Increase the Flow of Abundance to You

- *Abundance is mine. I am overflowing with riches. I am deeply grateful for the blessings in my life, which are . . .*

- *I have the power to choose positivity. In this moment, I opt to feel faith. I trust in myself, in the people around me, and in humanity. I have faith in the Universe and its infinite wisdom. Today, I have all that I need, and I know that I always will. I know that I can trust myself and that there are other people I can trust. I know that I can always trust the Universe, which has an unlimited supply of abundance and is always giving. It is giving to me right now! At this moment, wealth is manifesting before my eyes.*

- *I am a creative person. My life is a work of art. I approach it with creativity and curiosity. I am open to new ideas, people, and situations. I delight in discovering possibilities.*

AFFIRMATIONS FOR DISTINCTION #11:

Dwelling in Negative Emotions
Slows the Flow of Abundance

- *I love and accept myself and the choices I have made. I have learned great lessons, and I am continuing to learn even more valuable lessons. I am growing every day, becoming wiser and wiser. I am in control of my finances, and I feel great about the flow of wealth.*

- *My financial situation is healthy and positive! I am creating wealth. I am manifesting riches! I am in charge of my spending, and I use my abundance wisely. I give value, unconditionally, and I receive it, unconditionally.*

- *I trust in the Universe and its wisdom. I have faith that it is moving abundance around and providing all the wealth I need, when I need it. I open my heart and receive the wisdom and riches the Universe wants to share with me. I open my arms and receive the abundance it is bestowing on me. I am so grateful for the flow of money in my life.*

AFFIRMATIONS FOR DISTINCTION #12:

Your Desire to Help Another Become Abundant Creates More Abundance for You

- *I am grateful for all the special gifts that make me who I am. I love myself. I am rich, and I cherish being generous. I am thrilled to watch others experience love and abundance. It is thrilling to nurture others. I love to inspire people.*

- *My light inspires others. My abundance flows into the lives of those around me, and they share my joy as we experience wealth together. I savor each moment that I have the power to influence another to join me in feeling rich and teeming with possibilities.*

AFFIRMATIONS FOR DISTINCTION #13:

Your Gratitude and Appreciation for Your Own and Others' Abundance Causes You to Become Even More Abundant

- *I deeply appreciate all the love in my life. I am deeply valued and deeply blessed. I am rich with love and support. I am grateful for all the wisdom and resources available to me. I have a wealth of people who care about me and who enjoy seeing me experience abundance. I love to share my riches with them, and they love to return the favor.*

- *I have unlimited possibilities before me. I enjoy boundless resources. I have wisdom and common sense. I am a gold mine of opportunity and wealth!*

AFFIRMATIONS FOR DISTINCTION #14:

Your Abundance Will Show Up for You in Exact Proportion to Your Belief about It

- *I am grateful for all my opportunities for learning. I have tremendous wealth within me, and I am nurturing it, growing it, and cultivating it, watching it expand more and more and more. My love expands. My trust expands. My confidence expands. My faith in the Universe expands. My abundance is growing . . . growing . . . growing. My riches are growing . . . growing . . . growing.*

- *A rainbow of abundance is mine. The colors are vivid and extraordinary. My rainbow of wealth expands outward, filling the sky with all its many shades and hues. My abundance comes in every color of the rainbow: red and pink and ruby, blue and sapphire and turquoise, green and evergreen and sea foam. I am filled with gratitude for the riches in my life. The Universe blesses me with this rainbow of abundance.*

AFFIRMATIONS FOR DISTINCTION #15:

The Language of
Abundance Is Powerful

- *I love my lavish, luxurious, opulent life. I love my bulging wallet and the many figures in a row I see as I look at my checking and savings account balances. I love being a millionaire! I am a <u>billionaire!</u>*

- *I am saturated with riches that I share with the world. I love being able to write a huge check to my favorite charity! I love being able to give to causes and projects I truly believe in. I relish knowing that I am lifting up others as I share my tremendous wealth! I see their smiles and rejoice at their excitement and abundance!*

AFFIRMATIONS FOR DISTINCTION #16:

Ask for What You Want
(Ask and You Shall Receive)

- *I am a wonderful, loving, generous, compassionate, and kind person. I am worthy of riches. I deserve to be wealthy and to live a life of opulence and luxury. I am entitled to be filled with abundance. I claim my birthright to prosperity and wealth right now. The Universe is increasing my riches at this very moment.*

- *I appreciate my enormous wealth, and I am growing it right now. I am filled with joy, enthusiasm, and excitement as I work to bring value to the world. I enjoy the fruits of my labor.*

AFFIRMATIONS FOR DISTINCTION #17:

Your Unique Values Regarding
Wealth Are Important

- *The people in my life are gems. They are treasures and precious jewels. I am so grateful for their love, kindness, and support. I cherish the wonderful qualities of the people in my life. I notice and appreciate their unique attributes, just as I do mine.*

- *I love being able to manage and spend my money the way I want to. I am thrilled that I am in harmony with the important people in my life. Together, we make terrific decisions about how we are going to use our mutual riches.*

AFFIRMATIONS FOR DISTINCTION #18:

There Is an Abundance of
Resources Available to Everyone

- *I open my eyes, my heart, and my arms to all the resources and assistance available to me. I am patient and trusting as I watch the stream of abundance flow into me, its force growing stronger and stronger. I feel the rush of it pouring into my life from all directions.*

- *Every pore in my body opens to the abundance that flows in. I am grateful for all this bounty—for this river of liquid gold and silver pouring into me. I claim my wealth. I claim my riches. Thank you, Universe, for such tremendous abundance coming to me from every direction!*

AFFIRMATIONS FOR DISTINCTION #19:

Wealth Comes in Many Forms

- *The river of abundance is flowing into my life, surging with energy, and I feel it filling me up with wealth. It is wonderful to be so rich! I feel expansive! I choose to share all these riches! I open myself up to receive even more wealth.*

- *I am thrilled to be co-creating abundance in the Universe in so many ways. I love watching how the Universe works with me in our creation. I am inspired by its creativity! I open myself to all the abundance it is pouring into me. Thank you, Universe, for blessing me with this tremendous wealth!*

AFFIRMATIONS FOR DISTINCTION #20:

Right Now, You Have the Wisdom Within You to Be Rich

- *I am experiencing great abundance, and I revel in my riches. I take ownership of my wealth. I am the wise steward of my finances, the gardener who cares for all my riches. I enjoy learning about wealth, cultivating it, growing it, and sharing it. I value all that I have, and I nurture and tend my garden. I love to exchange ideas about increasing prosperity. I love to learn more about how to maintain my very healthy financial situation and expand my riches further. I have tremendous respect for all my resources.*

- *I have a treasure chest full of resources available to me at all times. I immerse my hands in its riches, eager to touch, feel, and experience my wealth as I imagine how to exchange it, grow it, and give it back to the ever-providing Universe. I am deeply grateful for all the incredible affluence I have.*

AFFIRMATIONS FOR DISTINCTION #21:

Wealth Consciousness Leads
to Wealth-Generating Actions

- *Right now I am aware of all the prosperity in my life. I am conscious of my potential to grow riches, and I am watering my wondrous, lush garden of abundance.*

- *I am committed to creating wealth. I am committed to honoring and respecting all the wonderful resources I have—to growing the seeds of my possibilities. Every day, I manifest wealth with my thoughts, feelings, and actions.*

THE 21 DISTINCTIONS IN 21 DAYS CHECKLIST

Use this checklist to keep track of how often you've recited your affirmations. Each day you'll make three *X*s in that day's box if you recited your affirmations three times in accordance with the program:

1. When you've said your affirmations in the morning, place an *X* in the first space in the box.

2. After your second recitation, which you'll do at some point during the day, place an *X* in the second space in the box.

3. After your third recitation at night, make a third and final *X* in the box.

Please don't quit the program if you start forgetting to recite your affirmations! Every day offers you a new opportunity to recommit yourself to this important program for creating wealth.

DISTINCTION #1		
1. _/_/_/	2. _/_/_/	3. _/_/_/
4. _/_/_/	5. _/_/_/	6. _/_/_/
7. _/_/_/	8. _/_/_/	9. _/_/_/
10. _/_/_/	11. _/_/_/	12. _/_/_/
13. _/_/_/	14. _/_/_/	15. _/_/_/
16. _/_/_/	17. _/_/_/	18. _/_/_/
19. _/_/_/	20. _/_/_/	21. _/_/_/

DISTINCTION #2		
1. _/_/_/	2. _/_/_/	3. _/_/_/
4. _/_/_/	5. _/_/_/	6. _/_/_/
7. _/_/_/	8. _/_/_/	9. _/_/_/
10. _/_/_/	11. _/_/_/	12. _/_/_/
13. _/_/_/	14. _/_/_/	15. _/_/_/
16. _/_/_/	17. _/_/_/	18. _/_/_/
19. _/_/_/	20. _/_/_/	21. _/_/_/

DISTINCTION #3		
1. _/_/_/	2. _/_/_/	3. _/_/_/
4. _/_/_/	5. _/_/_/	6. _/_/_/
7. _/_/_/	8. _/_/_/	9. _/_/_/
10. _/_/_/	11. _/_/_/	12. _/_/_/
13. _/_/_/	14. _/_/_/	15. _/_/_/
16. _/_/_/	17. _/_/_/	18. _/_/_/
19. _/_/_/	20. _/_/_/	21. _/_/_/

DISTINCTION #4		
1. _/_/_/	2. _/_/_/	3. _/_/_/
4. _/_/_/	5. _/_/_/	6. _/_/_/
7. _/_/_/	8. _/_/_/	9. _/_/_/
10. _/_/_/	11. _/_/_/	12. _/_/_/
13. _/_/_/	14. _/_/_/	15. _/_/_/
16. _/_/_/	17. _/_/_/	18. _/_/_/
19. _/_/_/	20. _/_/_/	21. _/_/_/

Distinction #5		
1. _/_/_/	2. _/_/_/	3. _/_/_/
4. _/_/_/	5. _/_/_/	6. _/_/_/
7. _/_/_/	8. _/_/_/	9. _/_/_/
10. _/_/_/	11. _/_/_/	12. _/_/_/
13. _/_/_/	14. _/_/_/	15. _/_/_/
16. _/_/_/	17. _/_/_/	18. _/_/_/
19. _/_/_/	20. _/_/_/	21. _/_/_/

Distinction #6		
1. _/_/_/	2. _/_/_/	3. _/_/_/
4. _/_/_/	5. _/_/_/	6. _/_/_/
7. _/_/_/	8. _/_/_/	9. _/_/_/
10. _/_/_/	11. _/_/_/	12. _/_/_/
13. _/_/_/	14. _/_/_/	15. _/_/_/
16. _/_/_/	17. _/_/_/	18. _/_/_/
19. _/_/_/	20. _/_/_/	21. _/_/_/

DISTINCTION #7		
1. _/_/_/	2. _/_/_/	3. _/_/_/
4. _/_/_/	5. _/_/_/	6. _/_/_/
7. _/_/_/	8. _/_/_/	9. _/_/_/
10. _/_/_/	11. _/_/_/	12. _/_/_/
13. _/_/_/	14. _/_/_/	15. _/_/_/
16. _/_/_/	17. _/_/_/	18. _/_/_/
19. _/_/_/	20. _/_/_/	21. _/_/_/

DISTINCTION #8		
1. _/_/_/	2. _/_/_/	3. _/_/_/
4. _/_/_/	5. _/_/_/	6. _/_/_/
7. _/_/_/	8. _/_/_/	9. _/_/_/
10. _/_/_/	11. _/_/_/	12. _/_/_/
13. _/_/_/	14. _/_/_/	15. _/_/_/
16. _/_/_/	17. _/_/_/	18. _/_/_/
19. _/_/_/	20. _/_/_/	21. _/_/_/

DISTINCTION #9

1. _/_/_/	2. _/_/_/	3. _/_/_/
4. _/_/_/	5. _/_/_/	6. _/_/_/
7. _/_/_/	8. _/_/_/	9. _/_/_/
10. _/_/_/	11. _/_/_/	12. _/_/_/
13. _/_/_/	14. _/_/_/	15. _/_/_/
16. _/_/_/	17. _/_/_/	18. _/_/_/
19. _/_/_/	20. _/_/_/	21. _/_/_/

DISTINCTION #10

1. _/_/_/	2. _/_/_/	3. _/_/_/
4. _/_/_/	5. _/_/_/	6. _/_/_/
7. _/_/_/	8. _/_/_/	9. _/_/_/
10. _/_/_/	11. _/_/_/	12. _/_/_/
13. _/_/_/	14. _/_/_/	15. _/_/_/
16. _/_/_/	17. _/_/_/	18. _/_/_/
19. _/_/_/	20. _/_/_/	21. _/_/_/

DISTINCTION #11		
1. _/_/_/	2. _/_/_/	3. _/_/_/
4. _/_/_/	5. _/_/_/	6. _/_/_/
7. _/_/_/	8. _/_/_/	9. _/_/_/
10. _/_/_/	11. _/_/_/	12. _/_/_/
13. _/_/_/	14. _/_/_/	15. _/_/_/
16. _/_/_/	17. _/_/_/	18. _/_/_/
19. _/_/_/	20. _/_/_/	21. _/_/_/

DISTINCTION #12		
1. _/_/_/	2. _/_/_/	3. _/_/_/
4. _/_/_/	5. _/_/_/	6. _/_/_/
7. _/_/_/	8. _/_/_/	9. _/_/_/
10. _/_/_/	11. _/_/_/	12. _/_/_/
13. _/_/_/	14. _/_/_/	15. _/_/_/
16. _/_/_/	17. _/_/_/	18. _/_/_/
19. _/_/_/	20. _/_/_/	21. _/_/_/

DISTINCTION #13		
1. _/_/_/	2. _/_/_/	3. _/_/_/
4. _/_/_/	5. _/_/_/	6. _/_/_/
7. _/_/_/	8. _/_/_/	9. _/_/_/
10. _/_/_/	11. _/_/_/	12. _/_/_/
13. _/_/_/	14. _/_/_/	15. _/_/_/
16. _/_/_/	17. _/_/_/	18. _/_/_/
19. _/_/_/	20. _/_/_/	21. _/_/_/

DISTINCTION #14		
1. _/_/_/	2. _/_/_/	3. _/_/_/
4. _/_/_/	5. _/_/_/	6. _/_/_/
7. _/_/_/	8. _/_/_/	9. _/_/_/
10. _/_/_/	11. _/_/_/	12. _/_/_/
13. _/_/_/	14. _/_/_/	15. _/_/_/
16. _/_/_/	17. _/_/_/	18. _/_/_/
19. _/_/_/	20. _/_/_/	21. _/_/_/

DISTINCTION #15		
1. _/_/_/	2. _/_/_/	3. _/_/_/
4. _/_/_/	5. _/_/_/	6. _/_/_/
7. _/_/_/	8. _/_/_/	9. _/_/_/
10. _/_/_/	11. _/_/_/	12. _/_/_/
13. _/_/_/	14. _/_/_/	15. _/_/_/
16. _/_/_/	17. _/_/_/	18. _/_/_/
19. _/_/_/	20. _/_/_/	21. _/_/_/

DISTINCTION #16		
1. _/_/_/	2. _/_/_/	3. _/_/_/
4. _/_/_/	5. _/_/_/	6. _/_/_/
7. _/_/_/	8. _/_/_/	9. _/_/_/
10. _/_/_/	11. _/_/_/	12. _/_/_/
13. _/_/_/	14. _/_/_/	15. _/_/_/
16. _/_/_/	17. _/_/_/	18. _/_/_/
19. _/_/_/	20. _/_/_/	21. _/_/_/

DISTINCTION #17		
1. _/_/_/	2. _/_/_/	3. _/_/_/
4. _/_/_/	5. _/_/_/	6. _/_/_/
7. _/_/_/	8. _/_/_/	9. _/_/_/
10. _/_/_/	11. _/_/_/	12. _/_/_/
13. _/_/_/	14. _/_/_/	15. _/_/_/
16. _/_/_/	17. _/_/_/	18. _/_/_/
19. _/_/_/	20. _/_/_/	21. _/_/_/

DISTINCTION #18		
1. _/_/_/	2. _/_/_/	3. _/_/_/
4. _/_/_/	5. _/_/_/	6. _/_/_/
7. _/_/_/	8. _/_/_/	9. _/_/_/
10. _/_/_/	11. _/_/_/	12. _/_/_/
13. _/_/_/	14. _/_/_/	15. _/_/_/
16. _/_/_/	17. _/_/_/	18. _/_/_/
19. _/_/_/	20. _/_/_/	21. _/_/_/

DISTINCTION #19		
1. _/_/_/	2. _/_/_/	3. _/_/_/
4. _/_/_/	5. _/_/_/	6. _/_/_/
7. _/_/_/	8. _/_/_/	9. _/_/_/
10. _/_/_/	11. _/_/_/	12. _/_/_/
13. _/_/_/	14. _/_/_/	15. _/_/_/
16. _/_/_/	17. _/_/_/	18. _/_/_/
19. _/_/_/	20. _/_/_/	21. _/_/_/

DISTINCTION #20		
1. _/_/_/	2. _/_/_/	3. _/_/_/
4. _/_/_/	5. _/_/_/	6. _/_/_/
7. _/_/_/	8. _/_/_/	9. _/_/_/
10. _/_/_/	11. _/_/_/	12. _/_/_/
13. _/_/_/	14. _/_/_/	15. _/_/_/
16. _/_/_/	17. _/_/_/	18. _/_/_/
19. _/_/_/	20. _/_/_/	21. _/_/_/

DISTINCTION #21		
1. _/_/_/	2. _/_/_/	3. _/_/_/
4. _/_/_/	5. _/_/_/	6. _/_/_/
7. _/_/_/	8. _/_/_/	9. _/_/_/
10. _/_/_/	11. _/_/_/	12. _/_/_/
13. _/_/_/	14. _/_/_/	15. _/_/_/
16. _/_/_/	17. _/_/_/	18. _/_/_/
19. _/_/_/	20. _/_/_/	21. _/_/_/

ABOUT THE AUTHOR

A *New York Times* best-selling author and an internationally recognized expert in the area of goal achievement, **Peggy McColl** has been inspiring individuals, professional athletes, and organizations to realize their goals and reach their maximum potential for the past 25 years. She is the president and founder of Dynamic Destinies, Inc., an organization that trains authors, entrepreneurs, corporate leaders, and employees in some of the most compelling and strategic goal-setting technologies of our times.

Peggy is the author of the *New York Times* bestseller *Your Destiny Switch: Master Your Key Emotions, and Attract the Life of Your Dreams!; On Being . . . The Creator of Your Destiny; The 8 Proven Secrets to SMART Success;* and *On Being a Dog with a Bone.* For more information about Peggy and her work, visit: **www.destinies.com**.

We hope you enjoyed this Hay House book. If you'd like to receive a free catalog featuring additional Hay House books and products, or if you'd like information about the Hay Foundation, please contact:

Hay House, Inc.
P.O. Box 5100
Carlsbad, CA 92018-5100

(760) 431-7695 or **(800) 654-5126**
(760) 431-6948 (fax) or **(800) 650-5115 (fax)**
www.hayhouse.com® • **www.hayfoundation.org**

Published and distributed in Australia by: Hay House Australia Pty. Ltd., 18/36 Ralph St., Alexandria NSW 2015 • *Phone:* 612-9669-4299 • *Fax:* 612-9669-4144 • www.hayhouse.com.au

Published and distributed in the United Kingdom by: Hay House UK, Ltd., 292B Kensal Rd., London W10 5BE • *Phone:* 44-20-8962-1230 • *Fax:* 44-20-8962-1239 • www.hayhouse.co.uk

Published and distributed in the Republic of South Africa by: Hay House SA (Pty), Ltd., P.O. Box 990, Witkoppen 2068 • *Phone/Fax:* 27-11-467-8904 • orders@psdprom.co.za • www.hayhouse.co.za

Published in India by: Hay House Publishers India, Muskaan Complex, Plot No. 3, B-2, Vasant Kunj, New Delhi 110 070 • *Phone:* 91-11-4176-1620 • *Fax:* 91-11-4176-1630 • www.hayhouse.co.in

Distributed in Canada by: Raincoast, 9050 Shaughnessy St., Vancouver, B.C. V6P 6E5 • *Phone:* (604) 323-7100 • *Fax:* (604) 323-2600 • www.raincoast.com

Tune in to **HayHouseRadio.com®** for the best in inspirational talk radio featuring top Hay House authors! And, sign up via the Hay House USA Website to receive the Hay House online newsletter and stay informed about what's going on with your favorite authors. You'll receive bimonthly announcements about Discounts and Offers, Special Events, Product Highlights, Free Excerpts, Giveaways, and more!
www.hayhouse.com®